James Smith

Professor Smith on the Bible

And Dr. Marcus Dods on Inspiration

James Smith

Professor Smith on the Bible
And Dr. Marcus Dods on Inspiration

ISBN/EAN: 9783337183318

Printed in Europe, USA, Canada, Australia, Japan

Cover: Foto ©Lupo / pixelio.de

More available books at **www.hansebooks.com**

PREFATORY NOTE.

THE following pages are substantially a reprint of a series of Articles which appeared lately in the *Aberdeen Journal*. They appear in their present form at the request of many friends who then read them. The author lays no claim to any *special* fitness for dealing with the subject; having been led to study it to some extent for his own satisfaction, he found that the main elements of it were within the reach and grasp of men of ordinary intelligence, whatever their calling or training may be. He professes to deal here, so far as Professor Smith is concerned, only with the Article "Bible;" and he trusts that what he has written may, as well as the whole controversy, tend in some measure to promote a better knowledge of the Word of God, and a more loyal and devout acceptance of its statements.

PROFESSOR SMITH AND "THE BIBLE.

The literature of the Old Testament embraces two periods—first, a period of religious productivity, and then, a period of stagnation and conservatism.

The first period extends from the time of Moses to that of Ezra, during which there was a continual conflict between spiritual religion and various forms of polytheism. The spiritual religion was compelled during this conflict to prove itself capable of growth and development, so as to vindicate its superiority to the false systems. In Ezra's time the spiritual religion triumphed.

From Joshua to Samuel we find a state of political disintegration and tribal jealousy, during which the worship of Jehovah was kept from being lost by the priesthood serving at the sanctuary of the ark. From the priestly ranks Samuel arose as a reformer to reunite the nation and revive the true worship. He did this, however, not as a priest, but as a prophet. (634 a.)

A priesthood is always conservative, not creative; but the spiritual religion could only live as a growing and creative power. It is the function of the priest to conserve the traditions of the past; it is the prophet who has the faculty of seeing religious truth in new lights. From Samuel's time the priest falls into the background, the prophetic ideas being distasteful to his aristocratic conservatism.

The prophet's work has hitherto been misunderstood in consequence of a twofold traditional prejudice—(1) Undue prominence has been given to the predictive element, and attention has thereby been withdrawn from the influence exerted on contemporary religious life; and (2) it has been assumed, in accordance with Jewish notions, that all the ordinances, and nearly all the doctrines, which are found in the post-canonical period were delivered by Moses at the very outset.

Thus the prophets were regarded partly as inspired preachers of old truths, and partly as predicting future events. But, in reality, they were leaders of a great development whereby both the doctrines and the ordinances were advanced from a crude and imperfect state to a mature and adequate form. It is only on this view that we can have a just insight into the prophet's work.

The laws of grammatico-historical exegesis applied to the Old Testament have proved the development theory to be the only true one, both as regards doctrine and ritual. Development in ritual has been less readily conceded than development in doctrine, because it involved a change of view regarding the authorship of the Pentateuch. But the facts are decisive. For instance, there is a manifest development of ritual shewn by comparing the following texts—Exod. xx. 24; Deut. xxxiii. 19; 1 Kings xix. 14; 2 Kings xxii. and xxiii.; and the last chapters of Ezekiel. (634 b.) The doctrine and practice in reference to "high places" are equally conclusive. Samuel and Elijah approved of the practice. It was exposed however to heathenish corruptions, and was frequently attacked by the prophets of the eighth century, under whose influence the high places were abolished by Hezekiah. But their abolition was not permanent. In Josiah's time a law-book was found in the temple and acknowledged by the high priest, in which the principle of a single sanctuary is laid down in accordance with Deuteronomy and in opposition to Exodus.

The indisputable conclusion is that the true spiritual religion was not complete in authoritative documents from the time of Moses, but was a growing system both in ritual and doctrine, and was propagated mainly by personal effort.

The priestly ordinances were mainly published by the oral decisions of the priests, and these were regarded as law (= Torah), and are so called up to the time of the Exile. It is probable there were written collections as old as Moses; but these, as well as the traditional ritual, were modified from time to time by the prophets and the priests to meet the varying exigencies of their own times. This is proved by the example of Ezekiel and the new law book of Josiah's time, which obviously contained provisions which had been no part of the law hitherto.

By the eighth century the prophets began to commit their teachings to writing, and these earlier writings were frequently cited by those who come after.

Besides the direct efforts of priests and prophets, spiritual religion was diffused in the literary products of the poets and musicians who had flourished as early as Samuel's time, and in the written history of the nation in which the theocratic spirit generally prevailed. In this history we find a *third* element—in addition to the priestly and prophetic—in the religious life of Israel, viz., the cultured lay element. Though generally the mass of the people were crass and unspiritual, there was a deep strong current of spiritual faith among them, as is proved by the fact that a man like Amos could be a prophet. Indeed, prophecy itself is, in one sense, the highest development of this lay element, which appears also in the Psalms, the Proverbs, and kindred works. (635 a.)

The captivity led to the triumph of spiritual religion. It was no longer possible to worship Jehovah as a tutelary god of the commonwealth. Those who returned from the exile had nothing left them but to obey Jehovah's law, and wait for the promised deliverer. This was recognised in the new institutions of Ezra and Nehemiah. The spiritual religion being now victorious became stationary and stagnant. The prophetic spirit had long been decadent, and it soon died, the national religion being now purely conservative. The sacred literature of the past formed the stay and guide of the leaders of the new theocracy. Ezra came to Jerusalem with no fresh message from the Lord, but with the book of the Law of Moses, *i.e.,* the Pentateuch, whose recognition as the rule of the theocracy was an admission that the religious ordinances admitted of no further development. The living prophetic voice now yields to the written canon. The tradition is probably correct which attributes the second part of the Hebrew canon, "The Prophets," to Nehemiah, who may also have commenced the third part. (635 b.) It was not completed, however, till long after, and seems to have been open to receive additions recommended by their own intrinsic value, or by bearing an ancient and venerable name. This is corroborated by the fact that the third part, the Hagiographa, held a subordinate position to the " Law " and the " Prophets."

The historical books form two parallel series—

(1.) The Book of Chronicles contracts the earlier history into mere genealogies, and dwells mainly on the kingdom of Judah. It is continued in the narrative of Ezra and Nehemiah, and the whole is the work of one author not earlier than the close of the Persian Empire. (636 a.)

(2.) The Pentateuch and the earlier prophets form another continuous narrative. These, however, are made up of a variety of different records belonging to different ages, and exhibiting many varieties of style, so combined as to form now a single narrative. The tradition that Moses was the author of the Pentateuch was mere conjecture. A Jewish scribe who regarded the sacred books as a complete history of Israel would naturally ascribe it to him, and identify other great leaders with other parts of that history. But a more careful examination shews this to be a mistake.

The Pentateuch was written after the occupation of Canaan, and Joshua is a continuation of it. (Exod. xvi. 35; Josh. v. 12; Gen. l. 24, 25; Exod, xiii. 19; Josh. xxiv. 32.) Names are found in it which were only given after the occupation—e.g. Dan, Hebron. The conquest is supposed as already accomplished, and even kings were ruling in Israel. (Deut. ii. 12; Numb. xv. 32; Gen. xii. 6; Gen. xxxvi. 31.)

It is futile to base any theory of authorship on the present division of the books. The history has not been carried on consecutively by successive additions, but is composed of several narratives combined into unity by an editor. Thus we find frequently duplicate narratives of the same events, and diverse laws on the same subject so divergent—not to say discordant—as to preclude the idea of one author (compare Exod. xx.-xxiii. with Exod. xxxiv., and the six laws about the Passover, Exod. xii. 1–28; Exod. xiii. 3–10; Exod. xxiii. 15; Exod. xxxiv. 18; Lev. xxiii. 5–14; Deut. xvi). (636 b.)

Astruc's famous discovery that two narratives, a Jehovistic and Elohistic, can be traced in Genesis, led to the discovery of similar parallel narratives elsewhere. The unmistakeable marks of the Elohistic author run through the whole of the Pentateuch and Joshua, though the exclusive use of Elohim ceases from the call of Moses. This document can be extracted complete, and its discovery is the great event of Old Testament criticism. The results of criticism shew that the Elohistic author is priestly, the Jehovistic prophetic, and that there is a third, a cultured layman, who has edited portions which are neither Jehovistic nor Elohistic. The story of Joseph, e.g., is very different from the Elohistic document, though it uses Elohim. This third author is a northern Israelite; but it is impossible to extract his contributions with accuracy. We thus find in Old Testament authorship the same three elements—the priestly, the prophetic, and the lay—which run through the whole Old Testament development. From the time of the Judges the priestly element becomes more obscure, and only the other two are clearly traceable. (637 a.)

The lay writer appears to be nearest to the events narrated, and on his record the prophetical narrative is based. Whether each narrative is by the same hand throughout, from Genesis to Kings, or whether each is the work of various authors shewing the same tendency, is uncertain. The date is also uncertain ; all that we know certainly is that these three narratives existed in Hosea's time, because they are clearly referred to by him.

A great controversy has raged regarding the third narrative, or series of narratives, i e., the Elohistic or Levitical. This controversy has turned mainly on some of the legal parts of the Pentateuch, such as Exod. xx.-xxiii., which is a fundamental sketch of the theocratic constitution, and the greater part of Deuteronomy, which is a development, and in some parts an alteration, of it. It is most probable that the writer of Deuteronomy was the editor of the whole history from Genesis to Kings. The style is certainly peculiar, and recurs in various passages all through these books ; still it is a style which might easily be imitated, and it may have been so by later writers. In any case, it cannot possibly be as old as Moses. Some episodes in the subsequent history are unintelligible, on the supposition that Deuteronomy was known to the actors. (Comp. e.g. Deut. xvii. with Judg. viii. 23, and especially with 1 Sam. viii. 7. Comp. also the laws about high places.) Deuteronomy is known to Jeremiah, but to no earlier prophet, and the whole theological standpoint of it is in accordance with that period. It gives the most spiritual view of the law, and if it be placed at the beginning of the theocratic development, the whole subsequent history is rendered unintelligible. (637 b.) The author puts his work into the mouth of Moses, because he is not giving a new law, but expounding and developing Mosaic principles. This involves nothing like pious fraud ; it was quite natural that he should adopt such a course.

If then the lay element was known in Hosea's time, and the prophetical element—comprising the whole of Deuteronomy and portions of the other books—belongs to the time of Jeremiah, the great question remains : To what period do the Elohistic or Levitical portions belong? These comprise the whole of Leviticus and the larger portions of Exodus and Numbers. There is no certain reference to this document before the exile, and critics are so divided in opinion as to make our whole construction of the origin of the historical books uncertain. The Levitical law gives a graduated hierarchy of priests and Levites. In Deuteronomy all are equal. Ezekiel xliv. shews that the hierarchical law was not in force in the period immediately preceding the captivity, and apparently never had been in force. There are accordingly two views of this legislation. The one is that the hierarchy—we might say the very idea of a hierarchical priesthood—is the latest development of the Old Testament law, and therefore the Levitical element is the last of the historical series. The other view is that the hierarchy existed long before the exile as a legislative programme, though it was never fully carried out till after Ezra's time. All the more elaborate symbolic observances are connected with the hierarchical idea, and hence the solution of the question as to the priority of Leviticus or Deuteronomy is essential to a right understanding both of the theology and history of the Old Testament, and this priority is as yet undetermined.*

How have all these elements been fused into one? In this way. The Semitic genius does not lie in the direction of organic structure. Part is added to part, and does not grow out of it. Thus the Biblical history is a stratification, not an organism. Anonymous writing and the utter ignorance of anything like copyright facilitate the process. A copyist adds and modifies as he pleases; he need not distinguish in any way between the original work and his own comments and alterations. He could compile a treatise by selections from various authors, and harmonise them in his own way. (638 a.)

Our present Psalter was compiled by making selections from earlier collections. The titles are of little or no value. The Psalms ascribed to David are probably taken from collections which really contained some poems of his. The authorship of two or three psalms may with confidence be attributed to David, but the greater part of them must remain anonymous. (638 b.) The 51st Psalm was obviously composed during the desolation of the temple. The date of the latest psalms is very doubtful. Perhaps the Psalter was completed before the latest books of the canon were written, or perhaps some of the psalms are as late as the Maccabees. We have no means of determining accurately.

The Song of Solomon describes the pure love of the Shulamite for her betrothed, and how it triumphed over Solomon's seductive wiles. Its object is political as well as ethical, and belongs probably to the early days of the northern kingdom.† (639 a.)

The Book of Proverbs contains, no doubt, many of Solomon's aphorisms; but we cannot be sure of the authorship. Some of them were collected by Hezekiah, who of course was no critic, and cannot have had any sure means of proving their authenticity. In fact from the variety of colouring it is manifest that the authorship extends over centuries.

Ecclesiastes was written long after the exile.

The noblest parts of the Old Testament are those of earliest date, such as the Book of Job, which was probably as early as the seventh century B.C. The author seems to have laid hold on an old traditional name, and to have attached to it the poetical incidents of his own invention for didactic purposes. The speeches of Elihu have been interpolated by a later hand. There is no reason why the same art may not be found in other books also. Jonah is generally regarded as an example; and some add Esther.

The poetical books, like the historical, are anonymous, and copyists have taken great liberties with them.

The earliest prophetical books belong to the eighth century B.C. Joel may have lived in the ninth. The older prophets did not commit their oracles to writing, and the writings we have are very much abridged, i.e. the oral utterances of the writers were much more voluminous. Some of the prophetic books shew a unity of subject and composition; e.g., Amos: others, as Isaiah, are composed of several books. Ezekiel appears to have

---

* So far as we can gather, Professor Smith has himself come to no conclusion on this point, but leaves it in this undecided state.

† Elsewhere Professor Smith says the deletion of this book from the Canon was providentially averted by the allegorical theory.

written what had never been spoken. (639 b.) Prophetic books were in circulation before the exile, and these were quoted by subsequent prophets; but by the time an attempt was made to collect and edit the sacred books many of them were lost; some of them existed in a fragmentary state only, and the authorship was not always known. Some prophecies have their authors' names, others are quite anonymous. They were all ultimately arranged in four books. It is not safe to assume that the authorship is always correctly assigned.

The predictive element in prophecy is simply the encouraging of the godly and the warning of the wicked among the prophet's contemporaries, by declarations of the righteous purpose of God concerning them.

The prophet always starts from present sins, present needs, &c., and there is no reason to believe that he ever received a revelation which was not intended directly and pointedly for his own time.

On this principle the latter chapters of Zechariah cannot have been written by him, but must have been soon after Hosea's time. Similarly, Isaiah xl.–lxvi. belong to the time of the exile, the author being some "Great Unnamed." (641 a.)

In Christ's time there was a learned and a popular literature. The literary party—the Scribes—had adopted a fantastic exegesis of legal traditions which were opposed by Christ. They made void the teaching and legislation of the Old Testament, but Christ came to fulfil them, to carry them forward to spiritual completeness Thus he attached himself to the Deuteronomic conception of the law. He saw also in the Prophets and the Psalms the image of his own experience and work as a teacher, and specially as the Messiah. The Old Testament bore witness to him in the spirit of its teaching and the mission of its prophets, and he recognised and accepted this testimony to himself.

The popular literature in vogue was full of apocalyptic mysteries and symbolic utterances, put into the mouths of ancient patriarchs, containing golden visions of deliverance and vengeance. These Messianic notions had become very crass and earthly. The new hopes of the Christians found expression in the revival of prophetic gifts, but the symbolical and the apocalyptic also remained, and these continued after the new prophetic spirit had died away. It culminated in the Revelation of St John, which is admitted to be of the Apostolic age, although its authorship is questioned and is really matter of no moment.

The Epistle to the Hebrews was not written by Paul, but by one closely akin to him; it may have been Barnabas, or it may have been Apollos, a man of Alexandrian training. Alexandrian influences are visible in it.

The Gospel of John is an unhistoric product of abstract reflection.

The Synoptical Gospels are a non-Apostolic digest of Apostolic tradition, both spoken and written, gradually compiled and arranged.

II.—CRITICISM AND CRITICS.

It is an axiom in Jurisprudence that Law has no passions, that it is no respector of persons, and that it moves in a region above the agitations to which mortals are exposed. In like manner Critics claim for their special department an entire exemption from prejudices and foregone conclusions.

Others are liable to be misled because they are ignorant of Criticism and are at the mercy of prejudices and "Idols" of various kinds. It is unfortunate however both for Law and Criticism, that while the abstract idea is beautiful, it cannot in this present world be anything else than an abstract idea, inasmuch as the law-makers and the critics are men of like passions with ourselves, equally liable to make mistakes, equally liable to have preconceived opinions and to have, consciously or unconsciously, adopted foregone conclusions. The history of Biblical Criticism since the beginning of the present century furnishes ample proof of the fact that the subjective element, the individual stand-point of the critic, his theological views, and other such-like considerations have a powerful influence in directing his critical methods, and shaping his conclusions.

The extent to which the subjective element has dominated critical opinions could scarcely be better illustrated than by considering the chaos of conflicting conclusions to which men—all professing to be above the miserable condition of having any forgone conclusion or dogmatic views to serve—have been led by their inquiries regarding the date and authorship of the Pentateuch. The time of Joshua, the Judges, Samuel, David, Solomon, Josiah, the Exile, has each been assigned. It has been cut up into two, three, four, or even more, different portions, of which one critic will have it that the ritual is earliest, another the historical, another the prophetic ; while editors, and revisers, and narrators have been called into requisition to remove all difficulties when the critics began to find themselves cornered.

It would be a deplorable mistake to suppose that at last the critics are agreed. They are as busy at the present moment devouring each other as ever ; and a new crop is constantly springing up to devour and to be devoured. And yet each has perfect confidence in his own method and conclusions ; *others* may be unscientific in their methods or illogical in their conclusions, but far be it from him to be so ! The history of criticism should certainly have taught its students caution and humility ; but it is doubtful if they have yet learned these lessons to much advantage. Professor Smith's article on the "Bible" is certainly disfigured, and its value greatly diminished by an unseemly dogmatism and unqualified assertion on disputed points on which critics as capable as himself, and with more critical experience, take a different view. Conclusions are said to follow indisputably, which do not follow at all ; facts are regarded as obvious which are very questionable ; theories and hypotheses are put forward as if they were well established conclusions universally accepted ; we are told all about how the ancient Hebrew authors did their work in an off-hand easy way, as if the writer had been brought up among them ; facts are spoken of as decisive which are not even facts, or at least very doubtful. Such expressions as these—" could not fail to be," " clearly made out," " appears most plainly," " the law was not dreamed of," " beyond doubt," " it is impossible to comprehend," " he naturally presents his views in the mouth of Moses," " of course a scribe would naturally leap to the conclusion"—all employed regarding matters by no means settled beyond dispute are not fitted to secure confidence in the methods, conclusions, or unimpassioned judicial calmness of the critic. To one who is not a critic it does sound rather odd to hear it coolly asserted in an off-hand way that Jewish Scribes would naturally leap to the conclusion that Moses wrote the Pentateuch, but now after three millenniums from Moses' time it has been discovered by some strangers and foreigners that their natural conclusion was based upon a mere conjecture! With all deference to the criticism and the critics, we must express our fear that it is too late in the day even for them to tell us all about the historical and literary conditions under which the Hebrew authors wrote, and to explain all the circumstances of the collection and transmission of their writings. Yet this is the task which Professor Smith set himself to accomplish. (634 a.) Considering how very scanty the literature of the period is, how meagre is the area from which facts and inductions can be drawn; and considering farther that the Pentateuch has to be brought nearly a thousand years nearer our time than is generally understood, in order to bring it within the range of critical artillery at all, we fear the critics will after all be obliged to leave it very much where they found it—in the hands of the Jewish Scribe with the name of Moses still upon the title-page. When even Sir Walter Scott could be deceived by a piece of contemporary authorship in his own tongue appearing under the guise of an ancient ballad, we suspect modern criticism can scarcely expect to succeed well with this task, when the data are a dead language, a few brief treatises, and intervening millenniums. If it be futile, as Professor Smith says it is, to attempt to base any theory of authorship on the present division into books (636 b.), how much more futile must it be for him to attempt a reconstruction of these books on a basis of a more reliable kind!

We are not at all disposed to concede the claims which Professor Smith makes on behalf of criticism and what it has done. In his statement or "Apologia" sent to the Free Church College Committee he does not hesitate to affirm that critical views of Israel's history make it far more intelligible than the old traditional view which frequently obscured the theocratic development which, it seems, criticism has brought to light. "Criticism tries to explain difficulties which the older exegesis sought only to explain away." If it *tries*, it can scarcely be said to *succeed;* otherwise how comes it that, almost without exception, the foremost men in the Free Church—Dr Duff, Dr Begg, Dr Rainy, Dr Smeaton, Dr Moody Stuart, Dr Brown, and many others, agree in regarding Professor Smith's views as calculated to raise difficulties, not to remove them? There are difficulties on any view, and there will continue to be; but it would be hard to point to any serious difficulty which has been removed by the upsetting of traditional views without raising more formidable difficulties in their place.

We are told, also, that traditional views have long hindered a just insight into the work of the prophets, which criticism is now enabling us to understand. But where are all these great discoveries? Where is the new light that criticism has created? Professor Smith's article gives none of it; neither does any of it appear in his statement to the College Committee. True, he mentions some difficulty which he seems to have had about the "high places," and which criticism has dissipated; but the ordinary intellect may be disposed to wonder where the difficulty is. But then the average intellect is probably not critical. He tells us, moreover, that similar examples might be multiplied; and yet, strange as it may seem, this solitary illustration is brought to the front again and again, and even when such a tempting opportunity was afforded him by the College Committee of multiplying examples and convincing *them* that he was right, he falls back again upon this solitary specimen! And after all, it is not tradition but Professor Smith that is wrong.

We believe traditional views are unwarrantably depreciated, and critical views unwarrantably lauded. No doubt it has happened that tradition has sometimes made void the Word of God; but *that* reminder would come ill from the mouth of criticism; and it is almost ludicrous to be told by Professor Smith that much unbelief has been produced by the old way of trying to reconcile contradictions, and that criticism has succeeded in arresting such unbelief by uniting the contradictions in a higher unity. Again we ask—What are these grand achievements? Where are they to be found? It is strange that no one appears to know anything of the great triumphs that the critics have achieved except the critics themselves.

We demur *in toto* to the assumed antagonism between what are called *traditional* and *critical* views. Professor Smith writes as if traditional views had no basis whatever—were a mere chaos which the critics had been providentially raised up to reduce to order and intelligibility. " Jewish notions " are sneered at as if, of course, they could know nothing about the transmission of their own Sreiptures. Who knows anything about these matters, who ever did or could know anything about them, but modern critics? It would surely be strange if Ezra and Nehemiah had not as good means of determining the age and authorship of the Pentateuch, or Hezekiah the age and authorship of the Proverbs as Professor Smith has. But the " notions " of such men are set aside by the flippant assumption that of course they were not critics, and had no infallible means of knowing. The critics only have that!

It would have been more seemly if Professor Smith had not so contemptuously ignored all criticism except that of the school to which he unfortunately belongs, It would have been little more than honest to have given some hint that there were still some critics whose views went to uphold the traditional doctrine on scientific, critical, literary grounds. It is known to the churches, although Professor Smith seems in blissful ignorance, that many of the ablest critics, men quite abreast of the most advanced rank of scholars, have their faith in the received views confirmed, and not overthrown, by their critical labours; and that if cricitism has tended to unsettle received opinions, criticism has also tended to settle them again. To talk of criticism and tradition as if they mutually excluded each other, as if any one who prefers the old paths could only do so because he had never studied the question, is calculated only to provoke a smile.

" It is a vulgar mistake," says Professor Smith,* " to assume an almost necessary connection between critical opinions and unbelief," in which sentence he quietly and, as it would seem, unconsciously substitutes the phrase, " *critical opinions*," for " *opinions of critics of the negative school.*" The College Committee had emphasized his agreement with the negative school; they expressed their regret, they called his attention to the fact that his critical opinions often diverged from those of " believing theologians;" and he replies that they are countenancing the vulgar mistake just mentioned! In other words, he contemptuously ignores the distinction which the committee carefully made between the opinions of "negative critics" and those of " believing theologians," as if the latter

* College Committee's Report, App. II. pp. 21, 22.

were wholly unworthy of notice; and, a few sentences farther on, this metamorphosis becomes still more complete by a farther substitution of the phrase, "sound criticism." *Sound* criticism is not associated with unbelief; as if the committee had said it was! Hitherto the subjective element, the character of the theology, doctrinal views, have really determined the critical conclusions. Believing theologians have not, as a rule, found it necessary to contrast criticism and tradition; negative theologians alone have done so. It remains to be seen whether Professor Smith is to reconcile the contradictions which have hitherto prevailed in a higher critical unity.

Notwithstanding Professor Smith's ignoring of the orthodox critical school, it is well for us to know that it has possessed and still possesses a continuity and vitality, a homogeneousness and unity, which we look for in vain in the other schools—or chaos of schools. Many of the conclusions at which the self-styled higher criticism has arrived would never have been heard of apart from the foregone conclusions of the theologians who arrived at them. It has been claimed for Professor Smith that he has forced into the service of the Faith many processes and results which have hitherto served only the interests of unbelief. We have failed to see what service the Faith has received at his hands; we have only heard as yet the shouting of the Philistines.

There is no fear that anything will be done by the Courts of the Free Church to "trammel the hands" of any of its professors in the prosecution of honest, earnest, critical study, or to prevent them from adopting such methods as may be most conducive to that end. But, at the same time, a clear distinction must be drawn between abstract theories about criticism and the concrete results of it. One may concede to the utmost the right of free speech, and, at the same time, have strong objections to particular utterances. It would be perhaps unreasonable to expect the critics to see it in this light, but it is really quite true that it might sometimes be useful —in the interests of criticism itself—that it were set free from the one-sided and unscientific opinions of its own omnipotence and sacredness into which its worshippers are so apt to fall. It is easy to raise a cry about trammelling people's hands, and obstructing the advance of thought, &c., &c. But in fact, if the engine runs off the rails, the sooner it is stopped the better. "The rails! These are just traditional views and ignorant prejudices of uncritical people; is criticism to be trammelled by them?" So we hear some of the critics exclaim. And we reply that, when the critics publish their opinions to the world, they must really submit to the humiliating necessity of having them judged by the "sanctified common sense" of the Church, and if they are likely to collide with other views which the Church holds more precious, there can be no harm in plainly telling them so.

It would be a pity if the opinion should be generally entertained that the questions involved, the results at which criticism arrives, are beyond the reach of ordinary theologians, and competent only for "specially equipped scholars." No doubt ordinary men are not qualified to carry out all the investigations needed to arrive at these results; but they may be quite able to understand them when presented to them. Men must necessarily devote themselves to special studies before they can make all the experiments and tabulate the results in any department of knowledge; but others may be interested in these experiments and quite competent to judge of the results when set before them. Must I be able to conduct an

Arctic expedition before I can understand the results which navigators have arrived at? Is it impossible for me to understand a scientific lecture because all the processes have not been personally superintended by myself? Are the gentlemen of the jury totally unable to give a verdict, because they could not have pleaded the case like the counsel learned in the law? Am I wholly unfit to consider or have any opinion about the bearing of critical results, because I have not myself made all the critical investigations? It is just possible that there may be hundreds of ministers and thousands of intelligent lay elders in the Free Church who are more truly qualified to give a calm judicial opinion upon the bearing of the authorship and contents of the Pentateuch upon the doctrine of Inspiration than Professor Smith himself.

The Church has no reason to fear criticism ; far from it. Critical examination—sound criticism—will assuredly confirm the faith of the Church ; it has done so in the past, and is doing so now. Like all science, it is the handmaid of religion and of theology. But if our Bible is so confused, our notions of its contents so crude and unscientific, our interpretations based on such ignorance and traditional prejudice, surely the critics are not serving their generation well when they have so long deferred the essential task of giving us a Bible freed from its chaotic confusion, orderly and intelligibly set forth, so that we also may be put in possession of this magic key which opens up all difficulties. Let the critics resolve themselves into a Biblical Revision Committee for this purpose. Meanwhile, when asked to receive with all deference the results of critical scholarship ; when told that we must not sit in judgment upon the bearing or tendency of any critical opinions, but that we must accept the teachings of these fully equipped scholars, we can only, with all humility, ask in reply—Which of them?

III.—HEBREW AUTHORSHIP.

We agree with Principal Tulloch,* that there are larger consequences in Professor Smith's criticism than he himself at present imagines, that his historic and spiritual sense have need of further development, and that he will probably learn by-and-by to state his conclusions with less confidence. We cannot, however, agree with the learned Principal, when he says that his article is admirably fitted to convey to the general mind a clear outline of the latest conclusions of criticism regarding the sacred volume. To our mind many of Professor Smith's statements are anything but clear. We have tried to form a conception of what the Bible is, according to the article, but can form only a vague, hazy, unsatisfactory notion of it. For this, to be sure, we may be ourselves to blame ; the article may be too deep for us. We are disposed, however, to think that we could see to the bottom of it were it less muddy than it is. We find in it a considerable amount of confusion and contradiction, expressions which are difficult to understand, not from the depth or greatness of the idea, which labours for expression, but simply from the unsatisfactory form in which it is expressed. What is meant, e.g., by "one

Contemporary Review, March 1877.

side of the assertion that this Gospel [John] is an unhistorical product of
abstract reflection?" or what is the "foundation of the theocracy in the
work of Moses?" What was the "new theocracy" founded after the
exile"? or what can be meant by the "ideal elements of the theocratic
conception"? It would surely have been possible for the learned Professor
to have put his thoughts into more intelligible language. It is not
improbable that he may have to complain of his sentiments being occasionally misunderstood; and we, for our part, reply to any such complaint
by anticipation by saying that his language is often far from easy to
understand. We must humbly and honestly confess that, on the questions,
"What is the Bible? and how did it come to be as we find it?" we have
found little new light; but seem rather to have lost any little that we had.

But we fear that the vagueness of the impression left upon our mind
at times as to what the author means or intends, arises in no small
degree from his own confusion of ideas, as well as the unsatisfactory
expression of them. In endeavouring to follow closely his train of
thought, we have repeatedly felt ourselves at one point come into sharp
and severe collision with a conclusion or an argument which we had
found elsewhere. Regarding the Psalms, "we have to begin by ques-
tioning the tradition contained in the titles. . . . There is no reason to
believe that any title is as old as the Psalm to which it is prefixed."
(638 b.) "The titles are far more trustworthy in the prophecies than in
the Psalms." (640 a.) Now, if the titles in both cases rest upon exactly
the same traditional authority, this arbitrary mode of rejecting and
retaining them does not commend itself as self-evidently scientific. The
arguments of the negative critics against the genuineness or credibility of
the New Testament books do not rely on external evidence, their
strength lies in internal evidence; but "the external evidence is as
strong as can fairly be looked for," and therefore Professor Smith
argues that the negative critics have no right to reckon this or that
book unhistorical or of late date on the ground of internal criticism.
(644 a.) And yet this is the very thing that he himself does in the
most arbitrary fashion with Old Testament titles, dates, and author-
ships. At one time there is "no reason to think," at another "no reason
to doubt," or perhaps "there is no reason for denying;" again, it is not
"safe to assume," and once more it is "a mere conjecture"—when in
sober truth, the matter of thought, doubt, denial, assumption, and conjecture is in each case to be received or rejected on precisely similar evidence.*

* This arbitrary method of dealing with evidence is characteristic of the Negative
Criticism. The latest example we have of it is in Dr Samuel Davidson's "Canon of
the Bible." In treating e.g. of the New Testament quotations in the Apostolic Fathers,
if he finds an awkward but undoubted quotation, he tells us that "all probability is
against" its being from the New Testament (page 92); or the reference is "invalid"
(page 94). If Papias speaks of Matthew and Mark, it is "most probable" that it is
not our Matthew and Mark (page 96), or "the matter is somewhat uncertain" (page
103). If the Fathers do not testify as the critics would like, they are "credulous
and blundering," or "passionate and one-sided" (page 121). As a crowning example,
take the following: "Whatever be said about Justin's [A.D. 150] acquaintance with
this [the fourth] gospel, its existence before A.D. 140 is incapable either of decisive
or probable shewing. The Johannine authorship has receded before the tide of
modern criticism; and though this tide is arbitrary at times, it is here irresistible.
Apologists should abstain from strong assertions," &c. (page 99). Strong assertions
are only for critics, and the more arbitrary the stronger. "No case: abuse plaintiff's
attorney."

" There can be no reasonable doubt that the priests possessed written legal collections from the time of Moses," but the " word Law (Torah) in writings earlier than the Captivity" means " oral decisions of the priests." Now, if you assert that the only writings which profess to be Mosaic did not exist till more than 800 years after, it seems very *unreasonable* to assume that there were other writings of which you find no trace whatever. And if you assume that there were such " *written* legal collections," how do you know that the word Law (Torah) means " *oral* decisions of the priests "? And again, if you find writings which mention the Law (Torah) before the Captivity, is it safe to assume that the Law to which these writings refer was not written also? There can surely be no reasonable doubt that it was.

As formerly observed, the law regarding high places has been the occasion of much critical anxiety to Professor Smith. He sees between the law of Exodus and that of Deuteronomy such a divergence or contradiction as to convince him that there must be a different authorship. And yet elsewhere he gives, in another connection, a satisfactory solution of his own difficulty, when he says—" For our present argument the main point is not diversity of enactment, *which may often be only apparent.*" For our present argument! Even critics can base their reasoning at times upon premises which they have no difficulty in seeing to be fallacious when looked at from another stand-point!

Professor Smith's assertions regarding Hebrew Authorship and Literature are given with a confidence and authority which no scholar can possibly be justified in claiming. The data for coming to an authoritative conclusion on such questions are far too meagre to warrant the dogmatism which is exhibited. But in addition to this, his ideas on the subject are extremely confused and contradictory.

The prophets, we are told, *began* to commit their oracles to writing in the eighth century B.C. (639 b.), and these writings were widely circulated among the people who " had attained a high degree of literary culture." Now, in Professor Smith's view, the prophets were far before the priests in their literary and spiritual activity, and we wonder how the people had attained this high degree of literary culture when the most literary and cultured among them, viz., the prophets, were only beginning to write. We suspect there is some mistake here, and that, if the literary culture of the Hebrews was what Professor Smith represents (though unfortunately he withholds all information as to the sources from which his very full and accurate knowledge is derived), their literature itself must have had its beginning much earlier than he and his authorities seem to suppose.

But while the nation was thus highly cultured, the writers, whose productions were the sources and constant feeders of that culture, seem to have possessed very little of it themselves. They had little idea of organic unity in their compositions; their genius did not lie in that direction. One man wrote a few sentences, and another wrote a few more, and another, and another, till an editor appeared, who transferred all these compositions to a single sheet, intercalating a sentence of his own here and there, and issuing the whole to the highly cultured nation, either as his own work, or anonymously! " If a man copied a book, it was his to add and modify as he pleased, and he was not in the least bound to distinguish the old from the new. If he had two books before him, to which he attached equal worth, he took large extracts from both, and harmonised them by such additions or modifications as he felt to be necessary." (638 a.) Again, we are told that the people and their literary instructors laid no weight upon questions of authorship; but the writer of Deuteronomy "naturally" put his work into the mouth of Moses : on what principle it is difficult to understand. If the people had no writing from the hand of Moses, and laid no weight on questions of authorship, why should the writer "naturally" do so unwarrantable and unnecessary a thing? No doubt, as far back as our means of investigation lead us or allow us to go into the questions of Jewish authorship, we find an unvarying tradition that the Pentateuch was the work of Moses, but how easy it is for modern criticism to dispose of a trifling circumstance like that :—"It is not probable that this tradition rests on any surer ground than conjecture." What possible answer can any uncritical person make to so satisfactory a disposal of the whole matter? If he should still wonder how the tradition arose, how the real origin of these books has been so wholly lost sight of till the modern criticism brought it to light again, the critical reply is obvious : "Of course a scribe would naturally leap to the conclusion that the Father of the Law was the author of the Pentateuch!" A very natural mistake for a mere Hebrew scribe! But modern criticism, having taken "a more careful view of the books themselves" than any Hebrew scribe could be supposed capable of taking, has discovered the mistake, and thereby shed a flood of light upon the state of Hebrew literature, the law of copyright, the want of organic unity, and the high state of culture generally! Ephraim especially possessed an unusual literary genius even among a people who had generally attained a high degree of literary culture, and yet for all that they laid no weight more than others upon questions of authorship, and were as incapable as their neighbours of distinguishing "historical data from historical deductions," which means, apparently, that with all their genius they could not detect historic facts amid historic fictions, or tell which were contemporary writings or which were a few centuries old.

If this confused and contradictory representation of Hebrew literature and authorship were correct, it would seem to supersede the necessity or use of any further criticism ; for it must clearly be a hopeless task to reduce the Biblical books to anything like order if this be a correct account of their character and composition. But, fortunately, it is not so. The very way in which, in the Bible itself, books and their authors are quoted and referred to, shews that whether their culture was highly advanced, or of a very primitive kind, they had some common sense even in matters of literature and authorship. If the Bible and its writers require to be dealt with in such a fashion before the "higher historical unity" can be reached—so much the worse, we say, for the higher unity, and the less we hear of it the better. It is said to be one of the fundamental principles of modern criticism that there is an organic unity in all history ; but if the records of that history be mere "stratifications," and if the writers had no genius for "organic structure" (638 a.), how are we to come at the organic unity of the history itself? Just in the way Professor Smith, and the critics of his school do ; we must somehow get into our minds a conception, an idea, or a notion of what that history should be, and then cut up the record into fragments and patch it together again so as to fit our notions. There is no other way in which the thing can be done satisfactorily !

This subjective method of dealing with history and the record of it necessarily interferes seriously with the essential judicial qualification of balancing evidence, which is quite a *sine qua non* in scholarly and reliable criticism. Professor Smith must either have been very one-sided in his reading on matters of Biblical criticism, or else he must have strangely overlooked many obvious considerations which would have materially modified many of his conclusions, overturned not a few of them, and led him to offer a statement of them all in a much less dogmatic form. In fact, we believe Professor Smith's whole view of Hebrew History, Prophecy, Ritual, and Authorship is contorted and erroneous. The weight of evidence on almost every single point is in favour of "traditional" views. We are not at present going to discuss the authorship of the Pentateuch, but let any one read the references to it in the New Testament, specially those by our Lord himself; let him then turn to Ezra ix. 11, which agrees with a law found in Deuteronomy; let him then decide for himself whether the former in behalf of the Mosaic authorship, or the latter against it, is the more conclusive. Yet Professor Smith tells us that "only a very strained exegesis can draw any inference of authorship from the recorded words of our Saviour," and he tells us * also, that the testimony of Ezra is so conclusive, that it can only be got over by being "explained away"!

To judge from Professor Smith's manner of stating the case, one would imagine that the documents of which supposed marks are found through all the books from Genesis to Kings, had been separated from each other beyond dispute, and that there is no longer any controversy about them : whereas the controversy started by Astruc in his "Conjectures," upwards of a century ago, is still raging as keenly as ever, and whatever way it may be settled, it has but a remote bearing upon the authorship of the Pentateuch. But how many separate documents are there? Are they complete in themselves, or are they merely fragments? What relation do they bear to each other? All these questions, and many others, are exercising the critics still; and, of course, as the decision depends upon so many subjective considerations, they are by no means agreed. The controversy about the separation of the documents has departed considerably from the old ground. Originally it depended entirely upon two names of the Deity, Elohim and Jehovah—hence the somewhat clumsy terms, Elohistic and Jehovistic—but now there are *secondary* marks (which, of course, are quite *unmistakeable* in the critic's estimation), so that the Elohistic document can be traced long after the exclusive use of Elohim has ceased. Then, again, the name Elohim appears in many passages which are not Elohistic, and as they cannot very well be called Jehovistic, what are we to do? The critics are at no loss what to do. "A third author is generally postulated for these sections," and thus the higher "criticism tries to explain difficulties which the older exegesis sought only to explain away," and this "new task is undoubtedly more delicate"!

Thus there seems to be little difficulty in doing for these Hebrew treatises, written at least five-and-twenty centuries ago, by the confession of criticism itself, what it would be impossible to do for a few pages of

* In a letter which he sent to the newspapers in reference to a statement made by Dr Moody Stuart at the March Commission.

well-edited contemporary English. Or otherwise, a little sharp criticism applied to Professor Smith's article "Bible" might, on the very same principles, cut it up into fragments and prove beyond dispute that it was written by three or four different persons, and that its traditional authorship is a mere conjecture.

The only other point to which we shall at present advert is the following statement about the Ketubim or miscellaneous writings not comprehended under the Law and the Prophets. This third part of the Canon, we are told, "was open to receive additions recommended either by their religious and historical value, or by bearing an ancient and venerable name. And this was the more natural, because the Hagiographa had not the same place in the Synagogue service as was accorded to the Law and the Prophets." We say nothing here of the very obvious bearing which such an opinion must have upon the nature and value of Inspiration, we merely call attention to the statement, in order to challenge its accuracy. Have all the latest writings been *from the first* classified as belonging to the third part of the Canon? Of course all Scripture is not equally suited for public reading; but parts at least of the Ketubim were read : Esther was read once a-year, the Psalms were sung, and other portions also were used. What is Professor Smith's authority for the statement that the third division of the Canon held a lower place than the other two? Is it in any writer earlier than Josephus? He knew nothing of any such distinction ; in his time all the Scriptures were reckoned of equal value ; they were separated by a great gulf from all other writings; they were believed to be divine, and "no one had the boldness to make any addition or change upon them." Is it possible that Professor Smith can trace back the tradition on which *he* builds no farther than the writings of Maimonides, in the twelfth century of the Christian era? He, we know, held erroneous views on Inspiration, and taught that the authority of Scripture was graduated accordingly, the Law being first, then the Prophets, and the third portion lowest. And Professor Smith, while setting aside as unworthy of notice, as mere "Jewish notions," all the most ancient traditions of Hebrew authorship which extend back into antiquity farther than we can follow them, has no difficulty in accepting as trustworthy, when it suits his "present argument," such a worthless invention as that !*

IV.—THE PROPHET, THE PRIEST, AND THE LAYMAN.

Professor Smith's Article on the "Bible" opens with the declaration that "the pre-Christian age of Biblical religion falls into a period of religious productivity and subsequent period of stagnation"—a division which will by no means commend itself to those who, underneath the letter, can discern the true spirit of Israel's history. The earliest of the Old Testament writings, according to Professor Smith, is not earlier

* Here, as elsewhere, we observe a marvellously close resemblance between Professor Smith and Dr Samuel Davidson, both in their views and expressions, which seem to suggest a common source somewhere. But the latter is obliged virtually to give up the inferiority of the Ketubim after a feeble attempt to assert it. He cannot get rid of Josephus except by saying that "his authority is small," and his language probably "exaggerated." (Canon, p. 57.)

than the end of the ninth or beginning of the eighth century B.C., and the latest is about the end of the fifth or beginning of the fourth ; so that the whole Old Testament literature in this view is confined within four hundred years. This period, we suppose, is what Professor Smith calls the "period of productivity," and the intervening four hundred years, from Malachi to Christ, constitute the "period of stagnation." But do these two periods exhaust the age of the Biblical religion of the Old Testament ? Could we not find, previous to the supposed commencement of the Biblical literature, periods quite as long in which the productivity or stagnation was equally manifest, though perhaps in a different form ? Is the writing of books the only mark of the vitality of religion ? Was there no productivity in the time of Moses, or Joshua, or Samuel, or David ? But, perhaps Professor Smith means the whole period of Old Testament history—not Old Testament *literary* activity merely—to be included in the so-called period of productivity. If so, we would ask, were there no intervening periods of stagnation ? Was the period of the Judges—say 400 years—a period of productivity or of stagnation ? Was the time of the Kings, from Rehoboam to the commencement of the literary period in the eighth century, one of productivity or stagnation ? How are the two periods defined and bounded ? Can we discover the characteristics and boundaries from the Bible itself, or must we call in some other witnesses to eke out the evidence ?

Running alongside this erroneous and confused conception of Bible history is an equally erroneous and confused notion of "Spiritual Religion," what it is and what it does. This is Professor Smith's account of it :—During the period of productivity, there was a continual conflict between spiritual religion and heathenism, in the form either of polytheism or a mere national political religion. During this struggle, the spiritual religion was forced to shew itself capable of growth and development, so as to prove its superiority to false religions : this conflict began in Moses' time, and continued till the time of Ezra, when spiritual religion triumphed.

Now this delineation suggests a number of queries to which, so far as we can see, Professor Smith supplies no answer. If, as would from this description appear to be the case, the period of productivity extends from Moses to Malachi, where are the products, what were the "ever clearer forms," what were the stages of the new development ? How are they manifested—say, in the time of the Judges and the earlier kings of Judah ? Were there no periods of retrogression, backsliding, departures from the truth previously attained unto ? Was there no spiritual religion before the time of Moses ? When or how did spiritual religion cease to be "militant" against *some* form of heathenism or idolatry ? Does not spiritual religion still need the Apostolic declaration and warning : "He [*i.e.* Jesus Christ] is the true God and eternal life : little children, keep yourselves from idols " ? And if it needed in Old Testament times to be "working out into ever clearer forms the latent contrasts between true and false religion," does it not equally need to be doing so still ? And, in that case, what bearing has this description upon a special criticism and critical understanding of Old Testament books ?

What we are told about the so-called "conclusive victory " of spiritual religion in Ezra's time is even more unintelligible and inconsistent, both with the truth of history and with itself. While spiritual religion was in conflict with Paganism, it had to bestir itself and prove its vitality by new forms to meet the ever-varying needs of the people. Hence the prophets arose as leaders of this new development; but after the Exile and Restoration "no political future lay before the returning exiles, and continued confidence in the destiny of the race was not separable from the religious ideas and Messianic hopes of the prophets. . . . With this victory the spiritual religion passed into a stationary state." (635 b.) Again, we are told that in the prophets of the Restoration "no important new ideas are set forth," and "the spirit of prophecy foresaw its own dissolution." Now this theory of the triumph of spiritual religion raises questions even more difficult to answer than the theory of its history and conflict. Did spiritual religion gain a conclusive victory because no political future lay before the returning exiles? Did spiritual religion prevail from and after the Restoration? If spiritual religion, forcing its way to victory, developed prophecy with its spiritual insight, poetic fire, and noble enthusiasm, how comes it that spiritual religion *triumphant* developed a set of third-rate prophets whose "tone of moral exhortation sometimes reminds us more of the Rabbinical maxims of the fathers in the Mishna than of the prophetic teaching of the eighth century?" How could spiritual religion give birth to a period of *productivity*, when its triumph and conclusive victory produce only *stagnation?*

Taking a conjunct view of what Professor Smith tells us about Israel's history and the spiritual religion among them, we are forced to the conclusion that this kind of spiritual religion is a very miserable production, and the less it triumphs the better; also that history and its development must be read in another way before any intelligent idea can be formed of them. The truth is that in Israel, as elsewhere, true religion had its periods of productivity and stagnation, backsliding and revival, not in two long stretches of a few centuries each, but in ever-recurring cycles of briefer duration, and that the history—as a spiritual history and a national development—is in this view quite intelligible to ordinary readers. The Law, i.e. the Pentateuch, is to the subsequent Old Testament writings what the Gospels are to the subsequent writings of the New Testament; and the view held by Professor Smith and his School that the Law consisted of mere oral traditions for more than six centuries will not bear calm examination, any more than his strange notion about the victory of spiritual religion. Few orthodox theologians or ordinary Christians would be disposed to deny his statement in the *British Quarterly Review* some years ago (to which attention is being called anew) that "the Prophets knew that Jahveh (*i.e.* Jehovah) was guiding his people to a higher standpoint in which even prophecy itself must fall away," but most of them would be surprised to learn that this higher standpoint was reached soon after the return from Babylon, when the spiritual religion was crowned with victory, and prophecy consequently first sank to the level of the *Mishna*, and then died!

The new teaching about the prophets, the priests, and the development of doctrine and ritual, is no more likely to commend itself to the general mind of the churches than the theory of history. Traditional views, says Professor Smith, long hindered a just insight into the work of the prophets, they were traditionally regarded as partly teaching old truths and partly foretelling future events. This view, we are inclined to think, is after all not so very far from the truth; and we fail to see any antagonism between it and what Professor Smith claims, most unjustly, to be a special discovery of the new critical school, viz., that the prophets spoke to the heads and hearts of their contemporaries, and that prophecy was not mere mechanical prediction. We fail to see in what way the "best thanks of the Church" are due to criticism, *i.e.* to Professor Smith, for bringing prominently forward a truth which nobody, worth hearing, ever denied; and we fail likewise to see how the new emphasis is "vital to the interests of living Christianity." We fear the learned Professor is somewhat inclined to over-estimate the value of his own labours and the results thereof. We are reminded here of an article of his in the *British and Foreign Evangelical Review*, an article full of learned quotations and references, in which he some time ago propounded a new theory of the meaning of the name Jehovah, or Jahveh, which was to have "important consequences for Biblical theology," and which turned out to be nothing more than a proposed substitution of "I will be" for "I am," as if that were a new discovery about the Hebrew tense! We have not yet heard of the revolution in Biblical theology that was to follow.

But we suspect Professor Smith understands his own view of the prophet speaking directly to his own time in a different sense from that in which it is generally received; otherwise we cannot see how he could consider it in any way opposed to the so-called traditional view. It is perhaps true that too much has been sometimes made of the predictive element in prophecy; but certainly it holds a distinct and prominent place in the work of the prophet, and did not necessarily grow out of the peculiar and special circumstances and needs of the nation at any particular time. The Gospel, as we have it, is intended and adapted for sinners in all circumstances; and the facts of the Gospel history, though long past, are still recorded directly for our time, and thus the record may be "a living word to him who reads it." Similarly the Messiah, Jesus Christ, was the Saviour of men in pre-Christian times, and the will of God necessary for salvation could not fail to contain some reference to His advent.

The Fall was the occasion of the first prophecy, which came direct from God himself, without the hand of any prophet; and all subsequent prophecy is rather to be viewed as the growth and development of that first promise than the growth of any element in Israel's history—that history itself being part of the larger development. This no doubt necessitates a more constant and absorbing regard to the *Divine* element in prophecy than has been shewn by Professor Smith; but if it be true, as he says,—and we of course cordially agree with him—"that that is not a true criticism which refuses to find in the Old Testament the special hand of a revealing God," it is no less true that that cannot be a true or adequate theory of prophecy which does not recognise the revelation of the Messiah as the primary and pervading element in it, and indeed the main object of it. We can therefore see no reason why Professor Smith should so persistently attempt to identify the new criticism with a true view of prophecy, or attempt to make the traditional view identical with making God's revelation "a mechanical, dead, unintelligible thing to the Church that received it." It seems to us that the more the Divine and Messianic element is understood to pervade all prophecy, the more life is infused into it, and the more intelligible it must be, in connection with true spiritual religion, to the Church in every age. Was the first promise a dead, mechanical, unintelligible thing to our first parents? Could the development and expansion of that promise be a dead thing to the Church in any age? Was not *the Church* born of that Word—the incorruptible and evergrowing seed—and was it not ever nurtured by the same? Is not the Word of God—the Old and the New Testament alike—a living Word to the Church of to-day? and yet surely it is not spoken directly and immediately to our time, in the sense in which Professor Smith seems to insist upon. The traditional view never made prophecy *less* of a living Word to those of the prophets' own time than to ourselves? Does Professor Smith mean that the prophecies of Hosea, say, were somehow more living and less mechanical to the prophet's contemporaries than the Gospels are to us now? No such distinction can be made; there was then as now the broad everlasting distinction between the letter and the spirit, between the natural and the spiritual man. And if the New View be so essential to a right understanding of prophecy, how are we to explain the book of Revelation? or how are we to account for the fact—for which Professor Smith is our authority—that part of Ezekiel's prophecy was never spoken, but written without oral delivery?

To be sure, " the prophet starts from present sin, present needs, present historical situations;" but surely an Evangelical theology has no difficulty in finding room for the most direct and explicit Messianic predictions in such a connection; nay, rather it would say there are no possible historical situations in which such gospel predictions would not be adapted to present needs, just as gospel preaching is adapted to them now. If the apostles preached Christ and him crucified as the wisdom and the power of God, did not the prophets do the same? Messianic prophecy —including types and ritual—was to the ancient church what gospel preaching and ordinances are now. To conceive of the prophets therefore as "partly inspired teachers of old truths, partly as predicting future events," is by no means to give an unworthy or mechanical view of the prophets' work. "Old truths" are what the Church has to live by in modern times, and it is yet capable of a great development in many directions through the living power of these old truths; and the ancient prophets, inspired by the Spirit, taught the same truths—old to a certain extent even in their day, yet ever growing and therefore ever new.

It is not a better, or a higher, or a more worthy view of the prophet's office to speak of him as "the leader of a great development," as contrasted with the view we have presented. It is a shallow notion, both of history and prophecy, which would make the connection between them, and the outgrowth of the one from the other, always manifest upon the surface. Thus Kurtz and others have argued against an exegesis which would find Messianic prophecies in the Pentateuch, on the ground that the organic progress of prophecy and its relation to contemporary history must be everywhere maintained, and that the Messianic idea is only to be looked for after the reign of David, in whom it originated. We do not know if Professor Smith would accept this particular application of his own principle, but it is a good example of how the principle may be used in the hands of critics who have a bias or a crotchet.

The same misapprehension of the true scope of prophecy pervades Professor Smith's explanation of the testimony borne to Christ by the Old Testament generally. He saw in the Prophets and the Psalms, He tells us, the image of His own experience and work; He recognised the testimony to Himself which was found in the spirit of the Old Testament teaching. But was that all ? He himself and his apostles teach us otherwise. On the way to Emmaus he found much more concerning Himself in the Old Testament than Professor Smith seems ever to have found ; and Philip appears to have expounded the 53rd of Isaiah to the Ethiopian eunuch after a manner which we fear Professor Smith must regard as uncritical. No matter, he was sent by the Spirit, and his mission proved entirely successful—a stronger argument for the soundness of his views than all that the critics will ever muster against it.

If it be true that the prophecy grew out of the historical situation, it is none the less true that the history grew out of the prophecy. Supposing for a moment that the traditional view is correct as regards the relation between the Law and the Prophets, it seems to us that any prophet or preacher, ancient or modern, might well be content to be used as an instrument in the hand of God for leading a great development in the practical exposition and application of the principles of the law. Certainly those principles—both in the moral and civil code—are far beyond anything which the world has ever seen practically exemplified as yet.

On any other view, we are left wholly in the dark as to what the " Great Development" was. What did it commence with ? What did it end with ? What were the steps by which its consummation was reached ? How did the one stage grow out of the preceding ? All this the new criticism must tell us before we can accord it our best thanks for the discoveries it says it has made.

The new theory of Israel's history and of the prophets' work being untenable, the theory of the priesthood must likewise fall. The priest never at any time became second in importance ; there is no antagonism between him and the prophet; his " aristocratic conservatism " was an honourable and virtuous quality, seeing it was the law and ordinances of God that he had to conserve ; and it was only when he became carnal, unspiritual, and indolent, that the prophet and he stood on opposite sides. We fear the spectacle may, even in these highly favoured and enlightened times, be witnessed occasionally of a man's personal character not being all that might be expected from his official position, and when that becomes general among the priesthood a prophet is required ; new life must come from without, when all is dead within. But from first to last— from Moses to Malachi—we find the priestly office in the front, and Israel's history must be sadly misread before we can ignore this fact. Why was Jeroboam so careful about having an altar and a priesthood— not a prophets' guild ? Why do we find the priests so prominent in Ahab's time ? Because, while denying the *power* of godliness, they were anxious to retain the *form ;* and the most prominent forms come therefore to the front. On Professor Smith's theory, how can we account for the fact, which he himself admits, that the law, *i.e.* the Priestly, Levitical, portion of the Canon, was compiled and closed before any of the others, and that " a complete body of the remains of the prophets" came only second ? If ever since Samuel's time the priesthood had become secondary, and " the priestly interest found little scope in the subsequent history," how could the Law take precedence of the Prophets in the Canon, both as regards time and place ?

Having thus disposed of the prophet and the priest created by the new criticism, we may at once dismiss the " cultured layman " without further remark.

It does not appear to have struck Professor Smith that he has himself put a fool's cap upon the head of his own theory of prophecy. The prophet was the leader of a great development both in doctrine and ritual. The two ends of this development we find in Leviticus and Deuteronomy. The one is the *terminus a quo* and the other the *terminus ad quem*—always bearing in mind that the cultured layman has prepared the soil for the seed. But which is which? which is the root and which the fruit? which is the beginning and which the end? Nobody knows; the critics have not yet decided. "Here arises the great dispute which divides critics and makes our whole construction of the historical books uncertain. As all the more elaborate symbolic observances of the ritual law are bound up with the hierarchical ordinances, the solution of this problem has issues of the greatest importance for the theology as well as for the literary history of the Old Testament." (638 a.) And this is the result of all the labour of the critics! Well may they exclaim, "Vanity of vanities! all is vanity; what profit hath a man of all his labour that he taketh under the sun?" But have they not rescued the prophets' work from the reproach of being dead and mechanical? Have they not discovered a new way of reconciling contradictions by uniting them in a "higher historical unity"? What matters it that the whole "construction of the historical books is uncertain," and that they have put them into such confusion that they themselves can make neither *head* nor *tail* of them? What matters all this, seeing they have made the grand discovery that there was a "GREAT DEVELOPMENT"? (See Appendix.)

V.—THE BOOK OF THE LAW OF MOSES.

The new criticism teaches that this book is a stratification, not an organic unity, and that its date is long after the time of Moses, that "the Law," prior to the captivity, means oral decisions of the priests. This criticism rests on very unsubstantial and shallow grounds. The negative critics generally—being anxious to establish certain foregone conclusions, and to eliminate the supernatural from Hebrew literature—are under the necessity of introducing hypotheses, for which it requires a total perversion of Scripture to shew any plausible basis. But Professor Smith was under no such necessity. He stated in his letter to the Free Church College Committee, that the authorship of the Pentateuch cannot be decided merely from "the few meagre hints as to the course of the critical argument" contained in his article. He does not, however, profess to adduce any original evidence or to have conducted the inquiry in a different manner from the negative critics generally; indeed, he seems to accept the "evidence which critics put forth" as being that on which he has himself decided the case. And this evidence must, on a calm and judicial review of it, appear meagre and unsatisfactory.

There are some things here which must be carefully distinguished. The *historical veracity* of the Pentateuch is not at all identical with the *Mosaic authorship* of it. The former may be admitted and established, though the latter be doubted or denied.

Again, the substantial authorship may be Mosaic, though a later editor be understood to have revised the work so as to allow of its being bound up and read along with subsequent writings. These questions are wholly different from the one before us. What Professor Smith alleges is that the Pentateuch is not in any proper sense the work of Moses, that it is the product of several hands manifesting diverse tendencies, that it must be arranged quite differently from the way in which we have it, and that it belongs to various ages all long subsequent to Moses. Each of these propositions is contrary to the evidence, and has originated with the subjective naturalism of the negative critics. We can merely give a brief outline of the state of the evidence.

1. We have abundant evidence that other portions of Israel's history were written by contemporaries, and it is *a priori* probable that Moses would have left some record of his own time. Samuel, Nathan, and Gad wrote a history, or histories, of David and his times (1 Chron. xxix. 29); Nathan, Ahijah, and Iddo left memorials of the reign of Solomon (2 Chron. ix. 29); Iddo and Shemaiah were the historians of Rehoboam's reign (2 Chron. xii. 15); Jehu, the son of Hanani, wrote the history of Jehoshaphat and his reign (2 Chron. xx. 34); and a history of the reigns of Uzziah and Hezekiah was written by Isaiah (2 Chron. xxvi. 22, and xxxii. 22), besides many other contemporary chronicles and official records. Part, at least, of the Book of Joshua was manifestly written either by him or by a contemporary who took part in the work which he narrates (Joshua v. 1, and vi. 25), and other parts of it—with Judges, which is a continuation—must have been written before the time of David and Solomon. (Compare Josh. xv. 63 and Judg. i. 21, with 2 Sam. v. 7-9, and Josh. xvi. 10, with 1 Kings ix. 16.) There is certainly then no *a priori* improbability in Moses also having left written memorials of his own time. He may have collected and edited such patriarchal chronicles as are contained in Genesis, and both these and his own work may have been again edited by a subsequent hand. There is a wide difference between an author and an editor; and, until we have some better proof than we have yet received, we must refuse to believe that such an obvious distinction was wholly unknown to the Hebrews.

2. The art of writing was well known in Egypt at the time of Moses. It was known even to the family of Jacob (Gen. xxxviii. 18-25). Moses himself knew it (Ex. xvii. 14, and xxxiv. 27). It was known to the Canaanites before the Conquest, who seem even to have possessed some sort of public library (Joshua xv. 15; Judges i. 11). There were various modes of writing and engraving known to the Egyptians at this period (Ex. xxviii. 9-11). This fact was formerly denied by the Deists and Rationalists, but overwhelming evidence was adduced to prove it. Writing, about a century and a half after the death of Moses, is spoken of as a distinct branch of business (Judges v. 14), and there was no reason to doubt that it was so from the beginning of Israel's national history. Letter-writing was a common practice in David's time (2 Sam. xi. 14, 15), and was known and practised also among the surrounding nations (2 Chron. ii. 11).

3. Throughout the Pentateuch there are frequent references to manners and customs which prove that the writer was intimately acquainted with the land of Egypt. Many objections formerly urged against the historical veracity and the Mosaic authorship of the Book on the ground of error in this respect have been completely set aside by further investigation of ancient histories and monumental inscriptions, and have—like most other

objections—tended rather to the establishment of the traditional view. Both the writer and those for whom he writes are better acquainted with Egypt than with Canaan; the age of Hebron is indicated by comparison with a town in Egypt (Num. xiii. 22); the fertility of the plain of Sodom is expressed by a similar comparison (Gen. xiii. 10); the manna is compared to Bdellium, which was well known in Egypt, but not in Canaan (Num. xi. 7); and the parties for whom the book is intended are constantly supposed to be familiar with Egypt. Trifling incidents are in this way introduced which on any other understanding are without force or meaning. This is specially visible in the history of Joseph. It is noted that he shaved himself before appearing in the presence of Pharaoh (Gen. xli. 14); that he formed an alliance with the priests by marriage (Gen. xli. 45); that he received a new name which has never yet been interpreted to the general satisfaction of philologists, but which the writer did not consider it necessary to explain; that he possessed a sacred cup (Gen. xliv. 2). Later we find similar Egyptian touches coming in quite naturally, and clearly shewing the writer's acquaintance with Egypt, while all references of a similar kind to any other country are wholly wanting.

4. That it is an ancient writing in comparison with most of the other books of Scripture might be inferred from the fact that not a few words found in it disappear from subsequent writings. The "gopher" wood of which Noah's ark was made is nowhere else mentioned, and it is impossible to identify it. So also the "garlick," * with which the Hebrews were supplied so plentifully (Num. xii. 5), is mentioned nowhere again. It is said by Herodotus to have been supplied in large quantities to the builders of the pyramids. A reference to a Hebrew concordance proves that the number of words found only in the Pentateuch is very considerable. We put little confidence in the results of mere verbal criticism applied to such a limited field as the Hebrew books afford; but it is well to know that, even on this ground, the marks of antiquity found in the Books of Moses are quite as numerous and satisfactory as the supposed marks of Jeremiah's time.

5. Moses, we are distinctly informed, wrote many things in a book at sundry times, and the Pentateuch is quite in keeping with such a mode of writing; and the fact that it was written at various times, in various moods and circumstances extending over a period of forty years, is quite sufficient to account for many of the seeming objections to the unity of the authorship. (Exod. xvii. 14 ; and xxiv. 4-7 ; and xxxiv. 27, 28 ; Num. xxxiii. 2; Deut. xxviii. 58-61 ; and xxxi. 9-24.) Many laws, e.g., are given in a brief outline at an earlier period, and repeated afterwards in a more extended form; some are given at first with special reference to the Desert life, and afterwards altered so as to suit the circumstances of their permanent settlement in Canaan. Or at one time a special law is given to enforce a particular principle of ethics, and at another time it is repeated for another purpose. (Compare Exod. xxi. 2-6, with Deut. xv. 12-18 ; Exod. xxii. 26, with Deut. xxiv. 6 ; Lev. xvii. 3, 4, with Deut. xii. 5-7.) This, as we shall afterwards see, has an important bearing on the relation of Deuteronomy to the previous books.

6. The other books of the Old Testament frequently quote the Pen-

* Of course we mean here the article of diet, whatever it may have been, expressed by the Hebrew word.

tateuch, and make constant reference to it as the basis of Israel's history and the ground of the prophet's appeals. Remove the Pentateuch, and the other books become unintelligible, and this not merely because *the authors of the subsequent books* had the Pentateuch before them, but because *the actors in the subsequent history* had it before them. The events recorded in the first chapters of Joshua, and onward through the whole history, are founded on the commandment of the Lord to Moses as written in the Book of the Law (Joshua i. 8). Now, of course, the *actors* in these events having the Book in their time is a very different thing from the *authors* of the narrative merely having it ; on the latter supposition both might possibly be centuries after the events recorded, but if the record contains true history, the Book of the Law must have been known to the actors themselves. The undoubted fact that the Pentateuch is quoted by the prophets of the Northern Kingdom, proves that it had been recognised by the whole nation prior to the disruption.

7. The universal tradition of the unity of the Pentateuch and the Mosaic authorship ought not to be set aside without the clearest and the most convincing evidence. Of *external* evidence in support of Professor Smith's conclusions there is not the slightest trace ; and, as we have previously shewn, the *internal* evidence is made to speak by the critics generally in accordance with their own subjective notions, and can be made to say anything, provided only the critic who for the time manipulates it be allowed a sufficiently wide range of postulates to start with.

8. The testimony of Christ and his apostles is entirely in support of the received opinion. We are by no means disposed to press, as some do, the mere mention of the name of Moses by Christ in connection with the Pentateuch as an end of all controversy. This *might* be explained, if it stood alone, without any irreverence or without derogating from the Saviour's divine character, on just the same principle as I might speak of Ossian's poems without in the least committing myself thereby to an opinion on the genuineness of the poems so called. The book to which I refer is best known by that name which conveys to the mind of the hearer a correct impression of the *book* meant without necessarily conveying any impression regarding my view of the *authorship*. The Pentateuch was known among the Jews in the time of Christ as the Law of Moses, and there was no other name by which it could be so easily and generally identified. Thus, when we read of Moses and the prophets (Luke xvi. 29, and xxiv. 27), we need not necessarily understand more than the books generally so called. Or again, when the phrase is " the book of Moses," it might possibly mean the book so called or the book *about* Moses (Mark xii. 26).

But there are references and quotations of another kind which completely exclude such a method of interpreting the name. We must bear in mind that there was undoubtedly a person called Moses well known to the Jews, and closely identified with their national existence ; that there was a book or series of books also called by that name ; that both the man and the book were held in extraordinary reputation among them, *and that the position held by each was inseparably connected with the position held by the other.* Moses was known and honoured mainly as the author of the law, and the law was held in honour as the law of Moses. Moses and the law are identified just as we identify Mohammed and the Koran. Then it is said, " The law was given by Moses," with the clear intention of emphasising the person—Moses being there opposed to Jesus Christ (John i. 17). Again, we read of Moses speaking in the law (John i. 45), and Christ himself adopts this mode of speech, "Did not Moses give you the law?" (John vii. 19); Stephen also builds a weighty argument upon the Mosaic authorship of the law (Acts vii. 22–53, compare ver. 38 with Deut. iv. 8, and Rom. iii. 2). Christ distinctly and repeatedly homologated this view (Matt. viii. 4, and xix. 7, and xxiii. 2 ; John v. 45–46, and vii. 19)—*i.e.*, he uses the term Moses to designate both the book and the author, and in such a way that he must mean Moses whom the Jews regarded as the author; and he does this in such a way as to make it manifest that *in his own view* there is no difference between the laws found in that book and the laws given by that man the author of the book. Or, to put it otherwise, Christ identified Moses and the Law just as we identify Mohammed and the Koran.

We know how sharply and unsparingly our Lord dealt with the traditions of the Pharisees whereby they made void the word of God ; we know, also, how unanswerably he met the rationalism of the Sadducees concerning the resurrection. The Sadducees acknowledged the divine authority of the Pentateuch, and that alone. Resembling in *this* respect the modern critics, they questioned all traditional matter, and would receive nothing which was not sanctioned by Moses. It will not be disputed that their respect for the book was inseparably connected with their veneration for the author. And when they appealed to Jesus about the seven brothers and the one wife (Mark xii. 19 ; Luke xx. 27), our Lord, instead of controverting their traditional view of the Mosaic authorship of the Pentateuch, clearly confirmed that view ; and that, let us repeat— not merely as designating a particular book—but as *identifying the book and the author* in circumstances when truth would have required him to dispel the delusion of his questioners, if it was a delusion. It is also significant, as regards the authorship of the Pentateuch, that while the Sadducees quoted a law from Deuteronomy, chap. xxv. 5, our Lord replied by quoting a passage from Exodus, chap. iii. 15, and speaks of their reference and his own as alike to be found *in the book of Moses* (Mark xii. 26), thereby adopting the traditional view of the unity of the Petateuch and its authorship.

Moreover David is quoted in connection with some of the Psalms in exactly the same way that Moses is referred to as the author of the Law, and this in circumstances where the argument demands that the personal king David be understood (Mark xii. 36, 37 ; Acts ii. 25–36). And add to all this that the man Moses whose name is thus used in connection with the Law is mentioned in the same writings in which such references occur as having appeared personally and had an interview with Jesus (Matt. xvii. 3 ; Mark ix. 4 ; Luke ix. 30, 31).

A better example of the frivolous and unsatisfactory character of the evidence on which the critics base their conclusions could scarcely, perhaps, be found than Professor Smith's flippant treatment of the New Testament evidence on this matter. "Only a very strained exegesis," he thinks, could draw any conclusion as to authorship from the recorded words of Christ ; and thus the whole New Testament evidence is at once set aside. He can produce much more satisfactory evidence—and that from the Bible itself—against the Mosaic authorship ; for does not Erza (ix. 11) ascribe a Deuteronomic law, not to Moses but to the prophets ? It seems that in his estimation one such incidental reference, when favourable to his argument, must be pressed to the uttermost, but that the mass of distinct and undoubted declarations of an opposite character is of no value! But what then does Professor Smith understand by "the prophets" in Ezra ix. 11? The part of the Canon so called was, himself being witness, not yet compiled. Does the phrase then mean *books or persons*? and if the latter, where is the straining if we suppose Moses to mean a person too? If the term Prophets was not at this time used as distinct from Moses, is it not much more natural to suppose that the Prophets may include Moses than that Moses afterwards included the Prophets, and that too at a time when the meaning of each term was distinct—"Moses and the Prophets." Was not Moses a prophet? And is not the term "prophets" elsewhere used to designate all through whom divine revelations were given (Neh. ix. 26, Luke i. 70, Heb. i. 1)? Had not the same law been reiterated from age to age by the prophets as well as given originally by Moses? And how does Professor Smith explain away the words of Nehemiah, the contemporary of Ezra (chap. ix. 13, 14)? How would he explain the words of Zacharias (Luke ii. 70) about the holy prophets "which have been since the world began," who (it may be mentioned by the way) are stated to have uttered directly Messianic prophecies? This method of dealing in the most arbitrary fashion with texts, according as they do or do not suit the "present argument," is quite characteristic of the self-styled higher criticism.

9. An unanswerable argument in favour of the unity of the law as given by the hand of Moses is found in the Epistle to the Hebrews, where the Aaronic priesthood, the doctrine of sacrifice, the tabernacle, and the whole ritual are made the basis of a profound discussion and made articulate with evangelical teaching in a manner which to the new criticism must be very perplexing. The unity of the law and its Mosaic origin are pre-supposed throughout, and a careful study of the whole epistle will make it manifest that either the writer of it or the new critics have made a grievous mistake.

We shall consider some of the arguments on the other side after we have looked more carefully at the book of Deuteronomy. Meanwhile we may remark that the Book of the Law of Moses can be traced from the time of Christ and his Apostles back to the time of Moses, and nobody ever heard of any other book so called. It is manifestly the same book which is called indiscriminately "the book of the law," "the book of Moses," and "the book of the law of Moses." This book, Professor Smith admits, is the Pentateuch in Ezra's time. The same book is expressly mentioned afterwards by Nehemiah (chap. viii. 1, 2, 18, and ix. 26, and x. 29-39) when the statutes, judgments, commandments, as well as levitical ordinances are those of Moses, and by Malachi (chap. iv. 4), who expressly declares that this law with the statutes and judgments was delivered by Jehovah at Horeb. This book of the law was well known to Zerubbabel and his associates (Ezra iii. 2); it was well known in the time of Hezekiah (2 Chron. xiii. 16), of Jehoshaphat (2 Chron. vii. 7-9), of Solomon (1 Kings viii. 53-56), of David (1 Kings ii. 3), of Joshua (Joshua xxiv. 26, and xxiii. 6, and viii. 31-34, and iv. 10, and i. 7, 8). Moses had commenced the practice of reading it to the people (Exod. xxiv. 7), and he had already commenced to write in it before reaching Horeb (Exod. xvii. 14); and the contents of the book are continually referred to in the Psalms and by the Prophets, when it is not expressly mentioned. But all this, which to ordinary minds is sufficiently convincing, is set aside by the critics as a " very strained exegesis, " mere " conjecture, " quite a "natural " mistake ; *they* have discovered a *new* way of doing " more justice to the principle that the Bible is to be interpreted by itself ! "

VI.—DEUTERONOMY.

What has been already said about the Pentateuch in general applies to that part of it called Deuteronomy ; but several things may be added in proof of its authenticity as a part of the Pentateuch, and a Mosaic document.

Prima facie the book appears to be Mosaic ; there is much in it which corresponds exactly to that period and to no other, while a few things which may seem to suggest a different period are capable of easy explanation.

1. The references to Egypt suggest the time of Moses. Any relation subsisting between Israel and Egypt at a later period—say the time of Josiah—was of a wholly different character. Egypt is throughout the book spoken of as the land best known, and Canaan as a strange land (*e.g.* Deut. viii. 7, ff, and xi. 10).

2. If the writer addresses his work directly to his contemporaries, then no generation could understand this book in that sense except the generation who sojourned in the Desert. It would require a great stretch of imagination to conceive a writer six or seven centuries later so completely identifying himself with the Desert period, and so completely forgetting all subsequent history, for

3. There is not the slightest reference to any person or period in Israel's history after the age of Moses (we are not forgetting the reference to Kings, chap. xvii. 14). There were many important persons and eras which a late writer, writing for his own age, would necessarily have noticed. There was a new departure in the time of David and Solomon, which is never lost sight of by subsequent writers, but which is wholly unknown to the writer of this book.

4. Events are minutely detailed which would have had no direct interest to a late writer or his contemporaries. Why should any writer make mention of the Emim, Zamzummim, and Horim, &c. (Deut. ii. 10, 12, 20, 23), many centuries after they had ceased to be, and make no mention of contemporary nations ? Is it after the manner of fiction to condescend upon such particulars as Deut. i. 1, 3, 6 ; iv. 41–43 ; xxiii. 3, 4 ; xxiv. 8, 9 ; xxix. 1, 8 ; and xxxi. 9 ? How can we account for the directions in chap. xxvii. about Ebal and Gerizim and the exact fulfilment by Joshua (chap. ix. 30–35) if these were not Mosaic ?

5. What explanation can be given of the benedictions or prophecies regarding the tribes in chap. xxxiii. if they belong to Josiah's time ? It is noticeable that the tribe of Simeon is omitted. At the time of Moses' death it had all the appearance of dying out, its numbers being reduced during the forty years' wandering in the desert to little more than a third of what they were at the time of the Exodus. (Comp. Num. i. 23, and Num. xxvi. 14.)

6. If Deuteronomy be contemporary with Jeremiah, why does the

writer of the former invariably speak of all the transactions connected with Egypt and the Desert as intimately known to those whom he addresses, while the writer of the latter as uniformly speaks of those and much later events as belonging to the times of the Fathers. Deuteronomy says *you*, not *your fathers*, (chap. i. 8 ; iii. 18 ; iv. 20, 37 ; v. 3, &c., &c.), Jeremiah says, *your fathers*, not *you* (chap. ii. 5 ; vii. 22, 25 ; ix. 14, &c., &c.), when referring to the time of Moses and subsequent periods.

7. The prophecy (chap. xviii. 15) is clearly Mosaic and Messianic. We have only to examine the numerous references to it in the New Testament to be convinced of this. It is referred to by Philip (John i. 46), by the five thousand (John vi. 14) ; our Lord himself probably had the same passage in view (John v. 46, 47) when he said, " Had ye believed Moses ye would have believed me, *for he wrote of me :* but if ye believe not his writings how shall ye believe my words ?" It is noticeable that in this passage there is a significant and designed emphasis laid by Christ upon the *writings* of Moses in contradistinction to his own *words ;* but if these writings were *not* the work of Moses, and if they had only traditional *words* of his, the argument here is meaningless.* Can anything be more conclusive than the language of the Apostle Peter (Acts iii. 22)? And if the " me" to whom the Prophet is to be like is not really Moses, can this quotation be defended on any ground which will yet conserve the infallible accuracy and divine authority of *this* passage of Scripture ? The same remarks apply to Acts vii. 37.

8. The admission of this book by the Samaritans and by all the Jewish sects as Mosaic is inexplicable on the theory of its being so late as the time of Josiah.†

9. The loss of all trace of its true authorship and the accompanying circumstances is equally inexplicable.

10. Deuteronomy is quoted and referred to in other Old Testament writings. When David arranged the priests and Levites in courses (1 Chron. xxiii. 4, and xxvi. 29), he appointed " officers and judges," the terms being identical with those in Deut. xvi. 18, and the appointment being in harmony with the Mosaic legislation in Deut. xvii. 9–12. Deut. iv. 7, 8 is quoted, 2 Sam. vii. 23. The law of redemption (Ruth iv. 5–11), in virtue of which Boaz married Ruth, is found only in Deut. xxv. 5–7 ; and in Ruth's case the custom was carried out exactly as it is there appointed. Deut. xxxiii. 2 is quoted by Deborah, Judg. v. 4, 5 ; and Deut. xxxii. 17 is likewise quoted by her, Judg. v. 8, the term חֲדָשִׁים *Chadáshim* in the sense of new or unknown gods occuring in both. Jephtha's answer to the Ammonites (Judg. xi. 15) corresponds exactly with Deut. ii. 9–19, and there is no other writing to account for his accurate information. 1 Sam. ii. 12, 13, by a slight change in the punctuation, might read—"The sons of Eli were sons of Belial ; they knew not the Lord *nor the legal right (or statutory due) of the priests with the people ;*‡ when any man offered sacrifice," &c. Being ungodly and

* Μωσῆ is opposed to ἐμοί ; ἐκεῖνος to ἐμοῦ ; and τοῖς ἐκείνου γράμμασιν to τοῖς ἐμοῖς ῥήμασι.

† The Sadducees, apparently the most ancient of the sects, did not receive as authoritative any books but the Pentateuch. As this fact does not suit Dr S. Davidson, of course " little reliance can be put " upon it. (Canon, p. 63.)

‡ The words in italics are exactly the same as those in Deut. xviii. 3, viz., מִשְׁפַּט הַכֹּהֲנִים אֵת (or מֵאֵת) הָעָם ; *Mishpat hakkohánim 'eth [me'eth] ha'am.*

ignorant they transgressed the law in such a manner as to disgust the worshippers.

11. In Deut. vi. 7 provision is made for family instruction and the transmission of the law from generation to generation. This is clearly referred to in Psa. lxxviii. 5–8. The word "Testimony" (עֵדוּת) there used is also employed in 2 Kings xi. 12, where we are told that Jehoiada gave to the young king Joash the "Testimony," with a manifest reference to the instruction of Deut. xvii. 18, 19. This was nearly two hundred and fifty years before the finding of the book in the temple by Hilkiah. There is no reason for restricting the meaning of the term to the Decalogue; it is equally applicable to the whole of the laws contained in Deuteronomy which all the people, and especially the rulers, were expected to be familiar with, as the above texts clearly shew. It was also to be read publicly at stated times (chap. xxxi. 10).

We may now examine some of the objections raised to the Mosaic authorship of the Pentateuch in general, and Deuteronomy in particular. So far as adopted by Professor Smith, they are (1) the mention of names belonging to a later age, e.g., Dan and Hebron; (2) the repetition—sometimes with divergence—of various laws; (3) the contradictory legislation about high places; (4) the mention of kings in Israel; and (5) the identity of the priests and Levites in Deuteronomy, contrasted with the difference between them elsewhere.

1. Later names. This objection is a pure mistake on the part of the critics themselves. Professor Smith mentions Dan and Hebron as examples. But at other times he is not slow to suggest *interpolations* as obviating all difficulties, and the possibility of such a thing has been by others suggested here. It is, however, quite unnecessary. Dan is mentioned twice in the Pentateuch (Gen. xiv. 14, and Deut. xxxiv. 1), and in neither case is it probable that Laish-Dan (Joshua xix. 47, Judges xviii. 29) is meant. It would have been out of Abraham's way considerably when pursuing his enemies in the direction of Damascus (Gen. xiv. 15), and it is geographically inaccurate to speak of "all the land of Gilead unto Dan" (Deut. xxxiv. 1), if Laish-Dan were meant; besides, the whole country west of the Jordan is included in the next verse. It is clear, therefore, that there was another Dan besides Laish. Even if Dan be placed at or near the sources of the Jordan, this will not at all suit the locality of Laish (see Judg. xviii. 29, and 2 Sam. x. 6), and this district, moreover, was already allocated to Naphtali (Josh. xix. 32–39). It is no uncommon thing to find two places, or even more, having the same name, e.g., Bethlehem, Kadesh, Hebron, Carmel, Ramah.

It is equally easy to dispose of Hebron. It has three names in the Pentateuch, Mamre, Kirjath-Arba, and Hebron (Gen. xxxv. 27). The name Hebron appears in reality to be the most ancient (Num. xiii. 22); in Abraham's time it was called Mamre after a man so named, a friend and confederate of Abraham's (Gen. xiii. 13); in Moses' time it was called Kirjath-Arba by the sons of Arba, the Anakim, who then had possession of it (Num. xiii. 22; Josh. xiv. 15; and Judg. i. 10). When Caleb got possession of it, he very naturally wished to abolish this heathenish name, and restored the original name, Hebron. The references given

מִשְׁפָּט had not yet so entirely lost its original significance as to mean an illegal or unauthorised innovation, instead of a statutory enactment. There is thus a verbal and accurate quotation.

above clearly shew that Kirjath-Arba cannot have been a very ancient name. The sole proof that Hebron was a late, or post-Mosaic name, is Josh. xiv. 15 ! One might as well say the place did not exist till Rehoboam's time (2 Chron. xi. 10.) The mention of the *three* names in the Pentateuch is an incidental, and therefore all the more striking, evidence of the Mosaic authorship, for at no other period could all these be so naturally and appropriately used.

2. The Repetitions of various Laws. The Passover, *e.g.*, is no less than six times enjoined with variations. But these are all capable of satisfactory explanation. Exod. xii. details the specific arrangements for the *first* passover, which was of course unique and *exceptional ;* Exod. xiii. regards it as a *permanent* ordinance, and connects with it also the dedication of the first-born, which, as well as the Passover, is based upon the redemption of the people from Egypt. Again, in chap. xxiii., the three feasts are mentioned along with other important statutes. In chap. xxxiv. the Passover and the dedication of the first-born are again brought into close connection, and more specific instructions given (ver. 20). In Leviticus xxiii. the three feasts are again enumerated, and more specific instructions given about the presentation of the first-fruits (vers. 10–14), which had been already enjoined in a general way (Exod. xxiii 19). The repetition of the law in Deut. xvi. needs no explanation. It supplies us, however, with another incidental and valuable testimony in favour of the Mosaic authorship of that book, for it is here only that the specific reason for using unleavened bread is given : "Seven days shalt thou eat unleavened bread therewith—the bread of affliction, *for thou camest forth out of the land of Egypt in haste*" (ver. 16). Now, what possible use could a writer in Josiah's time, *800 years after the event*, have for such a statement ? It is the language of a contemporary speaking to those who had taken part in the event. The repetitions are simply an example of the "line upon line" method of instruction, there is no contradiction, there is no development ; there are merely a few additional details or needed explanations.

This may be regarded as a fair example of the repetition of laws of which so much is made by the negative critics ; and there is really nothing in the objection but what a little careful thought would easily obviate. Even the double or triple repetitions of an historical event may be necessary in order that the historian may shew its organic connection with antecedent or subsequent history in different aspects and at different points. The history and legislation of the Pentateuch are so interwoven as to render their separation impossible. They form the warp and the woof of the whole work ; remove the one and the other falls to pieces. It requires no great penetration to see that during the forty years' sojourn in the Desert particular cases might occur which called for a more explicit statement of the law, and in particular that the regulations given in Deuteronomy when the people were on the point of entering Canaan, where everything would become permanently fixed and settled, would naturally differ to some extent from those formerly given when they had to modify all permanent statutes to suit the Desert life. Thus *e.g.*, in Exod. xxii. 26, mention is made of *raiment* received in pledge, and it is ordered to be restored before night, while in Deut. xxiv. 6, the *millstones* are expressly mentioned, and the receiving of them in pledge prohibited.

c

The principle of the law is the same, though the details naturally vary. We find the same method adopted by our Lord himself, in whose recorded teachings there are numerous instances of parables and precepts identical in principle yet varied in detail, delivered at different times. There is, moreover, a close connection, not only between the history and the legislation of the Pentateuch, but also between its ritual and ethical principles. The ethics of the theocracy form the preamble, the "Whereas" of the ritual, and in order to enforce these theocratic truths the ritual, which is the type of them, is repeated, so as to enforce the idea of the organic unity of doctrine and ritual, and to guard against the superstitious notion that the ritual itself, as a mere isolated arbitrary observance, possesses virtue *ex opere operato.* How needful such instruction was and is, the history both of the Jewish and the Christian Church abundantly testifies.

3. The law regarding high places. Briefly, Professor Smith holds that there was no law against sacrificing on high places till Josiah's time, but there is such a law in Deuteronomy, therefore the legislation of Deuteronomy belongs to Josiah's time. The law in Exodus xx. 24–26 does *not*, as Professor Smith asserts, "contemplate the worship of God on other altars than that of the central sanctuary;" and there is no contradiction whatever between this passage and Deuteronomy xii. 5, 14, and xvi. 16. Even if Professor Smith's view of "all places where I record my name" were grammatically correct, which is very doubtful, it simply implies the assertion of a sovereign right to choose, and *one* exclusive place was not definitively chosen till David's time. And, in point of fact, the passage in Exodus applies to the present Desert life, when the "place" was constantly changing, whereas Deuteronomy is contemplating the settlement in Canaan, where high places were closely associated with polytheistic worship, to which the temptation would become much greater than it was in the Desert. It is quite true that both Samuel and Elijah did not confine their sacrifices to the central sanctuary, but this is not difficult of explanation. The spirit of the law was always above the letter of it, and in Elijah's case the whole circumstances were so entirely exceptional that it is pitiful to adduce it in this connection. The law against high places was to prevent idolatry; Elijah's object was to bring back Israel from idolatry, and he was acting directly under the guidance of the same God who gave the law; there was no legitimate sanctuary in Israel, and obedience to the strict letter of the law was impossible. The moral and spiritual dignity of Elijah and his work, under the inspiration of God, was such as to render all mere ritual details of no moment whatever: the spirit is in this case all the more thoroughly conserved by ignoring the letter.

The case of Samuel is not more formidable. We might simply assert the obvious fact that with such priests as Eli's sons ministering at the Tabernacle the letter of the law might very well be dispensed with; and Samuel was acting under special divine guidance as well as Elijah, though his work was somewhat different. There may be more said, however, than this. By this time it seems to have been not an uncommon thing to remove the Ark from the Tabernacle and carry it to various places and for various purposes (Judg. xx. 26, xxi. 1–4; 1 Sam. iv. 3), the Tabernacle also, originally set up at Shiloh (Josh. xviii. 1), was afterwards removed to Gibeon; and thus the places where the Tabernacle and the Ark had been were reckoned holy, and retained their character after these had been removed (1 Sam. xxi. 1–6 ; 1 Chron. xvi. 39, and xxi. 29 ; 2 Sam. vi. 17 ; and 1 Chron. xv. 1, and 2 Chron. viii. 11). Thus the high places where sacrifice was offered were those to which the Ark or the Tabernacle was removed. (Compare the above reference, and especially 1 Chron. xvi. 39, and xxi. 29, with 1 Kings iii. 4, 15.) The separation of the Ark and the Tabernacle introduced a double priesthood for a time, and their removal from one place to another originated various high places which afterwards became liable to much abuse, and from the period of Solomon, when the temple was built, their use became an index of the spiritual state of the people. But all this implies that the law on the subject was well known. Samuel had, under special divine guidance, departed from the letter of the law in special circumstances in order to recall the people to a true perception of its spirit ; at a later period the letter was heedlessly and irreverently broken because the people had no regard for the spirit of it. Finding the authorised ritual profaned to the great scandal and injury of religion, Samuel fell back upon the more simple customs of patriarchal times, in order to conserve and re-animate true religion. Public worship is a divinely-appointed ordinance, and yet there may be circumstances in which, the form and the substance being divorced, men may become schismatic in outward appearance, and thereby manifest more truly the unity and vitality of the Faith. It is remarkably strange that an evangelical theologian should see insuperable difficulties in believing that Samuel, under divine guidance, could act thus, and yet have no difficulty in maintaining the new theory about Deuteronomy ! That the prescribed ritual was known to David and Solomon is manifest from 1 Chron. xxi. 28–30, and 1 Kings iii. 2 ; and that the spirit is everything and the letter wholly subordinate was also well known (1 Sam. xv. 22, 23 ; 2 Chron. xxx. 16–20). Many attempts at reformation were made, as by Asa, Jehoshaphat, and Hezekiah ; but the high places were not abolished, even the altars erected by Solomon for his pagan wives remained for nearly four centuries, when they were removed by Josiah (2 Kings xxiii. 13, 14). No one has shewn how the new law—supposing it *was* new—grew out of any special needs of the people at any time subsequent to the entry into Canaan ; the principle of the law was as clear then as at any other period, and throwing it forward into Josiah's time does not in the least help us to a better understanding of any thing.

4. The mention of kings in Israel. But the idea of a monarchy is manifestly prospective, and is by no means regarded with complacency or approbation. The general scope of the legislation contemplates a more primitive form of government. Compare *e.g.*, Deut. xvii. 9, with Num. xxvii. 18–21, where the mutual relation of the civil authorities and the priesthood are described in almost identical terms. The regular civil authority contemplated is simply a שֹׁפֵט *Shophet*, a judge, and the appointment of a מֶלֶךְ *Melech*, a king (Deut. xvii. 14), is purely hypothetical ; and we can see no difficulty whatever in supposing that both Gideon (Judg. viii. 23) and Samuel (1 Sam. viii. 6) had strong objections to the kingship when proposed as a practical step. They saw in it, in the form and circumstances in which it came before them, the rejection of Jehovah (Judg. viii. 23, and 1 Sam. viii. 7), and even if it had been authorised and contemplated in the law of Moses as a desirable change, they would have

seen at once that it never could have been so on that principle.* It is possible also that too much is made of the mere word "king," a title which is applied even to Moses himself (Deut. xxxiii. 5).

5. It is said that in Deuteronomy the priests and Levites are identical, which proves a progressive development and change of view regarding the priesthood. The objection is frivolous and ill-founded. Certainly the priests, whoever they were, are as prominent in Deuteronomy as elsewhere, which ill agrees with Professor Smith's other notion that long before Josiah's time they had fallen into the shade.

But (1.) Deuteronomy xviii. 1–8 clearly proves that the distinction between priests and other Levites was not obliterated but rather confirmed.

(2.) After the book was found by Hilkiah in the temple, the priests and Levites were as distinct as before; the Levites who were not priests were to be the teachers of the people (2 Chron. xxx. 22, and xxxv. 3; Deut. xxxiii. 10). Hezekiah, who had formerly made a reformation very similar to Josiah's, carried out this regulation, and so also did Jehoshaphat (2 Chron. xvii. 9). Deut. xxxiii. 10 therefore introduced no new legislation.

(3.) The way in which the priests and Levites are spoken of at the coronation of Joash (comp. 2 Kings xi. and 2 Chron. xxiii), and also at the dedication of the temple, shews that there is no special emphasis to be put upon the expression, "the priests the Levites." According to the new criticism, the distinction made in 1 Kings viii. 4 (comp. 2 Chron. v. 5) is a mistake.

(4.) The emphasizing of *Levitical* priests is in perfect accordance with the transition period to which Deuteronomy belongs. Like many other of the Mosaic laws, those regarding the priesthood had not been strictly adhered to in the Desert, but henceforth no priests can be allowed to minister but those of the tribe of Levi and the family of Aaron.

(5.) The expression, "priests *and* Levites," is used by Ezra and Nehemiah (*passim*), and the distinction clearly marked. The expression, "the priests the Levites," is once used by Nehemiah (chap. xi. 20); it occurs also in Josh. iii. 3, and therefore proves nothing.

(6.) The division of the priests and Levites into courses by David (1 Chron. xxi. 24–29, and xxiii. 6) was continued by Solomon (2 Chron. viii. 14) and Hezekiah (2 Chron. xxxi. 17–21). The same arrangement subsisted in the time of Josiah, Ezra, &c., down to the time of Christ (Luke i. 5–8). The Deuteronomic legislation, which according to the critics revolutionised the priesthood, left all these things unchanged! The fact is that the Aaronic priesthood, instituted in the Desert, was the only divinely instituted or authorised priesthood ever existing in Israel, and there is no proof of any other.

(7.) In the Epistle to the Hebrews (chap. vii. 11) the expression, "Levitical priesthood," is used as synonymous with "the order of Aaron" (comp. chap. v. 4), and is contrasted with that of Melchisedec. It is also argued that the priesthood, which has always been an essential element in true worship, must be expressly appointed by God (chap. v. 4), and that any change in it indicates an entire revolution in the whole economy (chap vii. 11–18). Now the critics are bound to shew when, where, and for what important purpose the change which they insist upon was made.

* "The land of his possession" (Deut. ii. 12), may be applied to the country east of Jordan merely as in chap. iii. 20, Josh. i. 15, and xii. 6.

VII.—THE PERSONATION THEORY.

Professor Smith's idea about Deuteronomy is this. It is a development of the Mosaic legislation belonging to the time of Josiah, containing the oracles of some unknown prophet of that period who put his own work into the mouth of Moses. We have already demonstrated that there is no necessity for such a theory, and that it does not in the least help us to understand anything better than we did before. We shall now shew that it is utterly untenable.

1. Professor Smith says it was *natural* for the author to use Moses' name, on what ground unfortunately he does not say. He says also that in doing so he adopted a "literary method" which was quite usual; it was, in fact, "a liberty common to every historian of antiquity,"* and consisted merely in throwing "certain didactic matter into the form of a speech." Now, in opposition to this bold declaration, we affirm that such a proceeding as this would have been most *unnatural*, and that no parallel case can be adduced from either ancient or modern literature. For what is the true state of the case? Is it *merely* certain didactic matter in the form of a speech? According to his own shewing, it is much more than this. A book is accidentally discovered, written nobody knows when, where, or by whom. It is, without the least inquiry, accepted as a divine authoritative law-book. The king and all the people are greatly troubled because neither they nor their fathers had kept the word of the Lord as contained in that book (2 Chron. xxxiv. 21), although of course neither they nor their fathers had ever heard of it before or had any opportunity of knowing its contents. And besides all this, much evil and many curses were to come upon them for not keeping a law which it was impossible they could have ever heard of. Well may we ask, in Professor Smith's own words, "Can it be denied that to many minds such a circumstance must appear to suggest a far more fundamental difficulty" than any that it professes to remove?

But farther, the author of this new law-book is never heard of. Professor Smith says everybody knew quite well what it was, but really we must ask where he got his information. When we read the thirty-fourth and thirty-fifth chapters of Second Chronicles, we must confess that we naturally suppose that this was a book which had been well known to exist, that everybody at once understood what book it was, and that if Professor Smith be right, Josiah and all concerned were labouring under some egregious mistake. The whole thing is utterly unnatural.

But it is a sort of thing, we are told, which was done by all ancient historians. In order to produce a parallel case, Professor Smith must bring forward one in which an unknown author uses the name of a legislator who lived eight centuries before, a man of great renown, on the title page of his own production, wherein he introduces new legislation to supersede the old; he must shew further that a nation has at once, without the least inquiry, accepted the new legislation and been thrown into a state of great alarm because their fathers had not obeyed it; and, finally, he must be able to prove that there has from the earliest times been a universal tradition that the work was really the work of him whose name it bore. Until this can be done, it is simply ridiculous to talk about a

* "Remarks," in App. II. Coll. Com. Report, p. 23.

" liberty common to every historian of antiquity." It is impossible to argue the case, if this book, bearing to be historical, professing to relate the intercourse between Moses and Israel, and in every respect accordant with that profession, whose character is not didactic merely, but historical and legislative also, is to be dealt with as a mere dramatic fiction. If *that* is all that criticism can do for the Bible and us, instead of according it our best thanks for its valuable services, as Professor Smith thinks we should, we would gladly give it hearty thanks to let the Bible alone and try its skill on some *corpus vile* on which it might experiment undisturbed.

2. But unless we suppose Deuteronomy to belong to Josiah's time, our " uncritical tradition " obscures " the order and regular progress " of God's dealings with Israel. *i.e.* the great development which the critics have discovered. Now, we must repeat what we have substantially said before, that this idea, as they understand it, is a pure imagination ; there is in the Old Testament ritual no such development as they profess to have discovered. The mere ritual is nothing in itself, apart from the ethical and spiritual truths of which it is the expression ; separated from these, it is purely arbitrary and changeable, not fixed and determinate. There was, undoubtedly, a great deal of meaning in the Jewish ritual, which was probably never rightly understood ; we believe there was much in it which even now is not understood ; and the real development consisted in the deeper study, the better understanding, and the more intelligent and spiritual practice both of the moral and Levitical laws. Both the ethical and the ritual contained an *ideal* toward which Israel was to be educated and disciplined, as well as the germs and living roots from which that education and discipline was to spring.

Now, in order to prove their theory of a great development of ritual, the critics would require to show what is the mutual relation between the ritual and the ethic at every step, how they grow out of each other, and how the one as it grows is adapted at each new phase to express the simultaneous growth of the other. It may fairly be a question whether a development of ritual, having a true spiritual significance, would not be a simplification and a curtailing of forms and precepts rather than otherwise ; for as the truly spiritual is apprehended and becomes operative in forming the thoughts and habits, the less need is there for the ritual, which is to a certain extent a scaffolding for the spiritual building, an artificial support for the spiritual plant.

If, in this light, we regard the legislation about high places, we can see no reason why the permission should have been first and the prohibition last, as Professor Smith maintains ; and it is for him to show us in what respect Israel had reached a stage of development in the time of Josiah in connection with which this particular prohibition becomes so expressive, and that at any previous period it would have been *mal apropos*. We would, if compelled to take a side, rather argue the opposite, for spiritual development throws off the ritualistic yoke, positive injunctions are more safely dispensed with, and the permission to sacrifice on high places might plausibly be regarded as an intermediate stage between the restriction of all sacrifice to one place and the throwing down of all partitions, when the whole earth might become a place for worship of the highest, the most spiritual, and least ritualistic kind.

As we have previously shewn, the great difference between Leviticus and Deuteronomy in the matter of legislation is, that the former has respect to the present Wilderness life, and the latter contemplates the people as dwelling in Canaan. Add to this the explanations and details which forty years' experience as supreme judge in explaining all the difficulties and settling all controversies had suggested ; add further the spiritual progress and the literary experience of the author during the same period, and you have an entirely satisfactory explanation of the supposed differences in style and divergencies of legislation found in them. Deuteronomy has no specific reference or adaptation to any definite period of Israel's history; it simply contemplates them, in the most general manner, as settled in the land of Canaan.

3. How does Professor Smith's theory agree with the contents of the book itself? The work is put into the mouth of Moses; but that is not all. We might suppose Moses to rise from the dead and deliver a divine message to the men of this generation ; we might suppose a cultured clever author to deliver in the name of Moses such a message as we might anticipate—a message applying the precepts of the Decalogue to the conscience and life of this age. And Professor Smith seems to think that that is something like what the author of Deuteronomy did. But it is entirely the reverse. The author does not bring Moses up to speak to the Israel of the seventh century B.C., but he himself goes back and speaks exactly as Moses might have been supposed to speak to the Israel of the fifteenth ! Some one has sought an illustration of the state of the case from the supposition that Carlyle, being an ardent Republican, had issued, under the title of letters and speeches by Oliver Cromwell, a work of his own, inculcating republican sentiments ; and this has been regarded as a parallel case. But if Carlyle had really wanted us to hear what Oliver Cromwell would have to say to us, is it conceivable that he would have clothed his utterances in the antiquated language and phraseology of the sixteenth century, that he would at once have introduced all the manners and customs of that age instead of ours, that he would have intertwined his republican doctrine inextricably with the history of the Civil War, that he would have utterly ignored all that has happened since, that he would have written it so completely with the effect of making us acquainted with Cromwell's times, when his real object was to make Cromwell speak directly to us and our times? For he is a contemporary author, and there is no reason to think that he would speak otherwise than directly and pointedly to his own time—i.e., to us, for our development. But its use as an illustration is this :—As Carlyle could not possibly have concocted these letters and speeches as Oliver Cromwell's with the view of inculcating republican views on this nineteenth century, but would of necessity, as a reasonable being, have adopted a totally different method, so the author of Deuteronomy could not possibly have put his work into the mouth of Moses in the form in which it is, while he intended it all the time to be a direct and pointed appeal to Israel in the seventh century. Moreover, the history given us in " Cromwell's Letters and Speeches," is known from other sources to be true history, whereas the author of Deuteronomy falsifies history,—or, let us say, makes a historical romance, as a framework for his didactic and legislative matter. The more the subject is calmly considered, the more irresistible will the conclusion be that Deuteronomy is no more a romance of the sixth century B.C., than Cromwell's Letters are a fiction of this nineteenth century A.D.

If we could imagine some prophetical genius of the present time publishing an historical romance pertaining to the time of the Norman Conquest, under the name of William the Conqueror, containing new principles of legislation, which at once creates immense excitement in the political and religious world, and leads to the immediate enforcing of the suggested laws, while everybody knows that it is a romance by a living author; if we could suppose farther, that in a few generations from the present time this book will come in some unaccountable way to be accepted as really historical, and to be *bona fide* the law book introduced into England by the Conqueror, we would have some approach to the absurdity under consideration : with this important exception that, in the estimation of *some* of the critics, the Jewish author was inspired by the Holy Ghost!

4. We must have some more definite information about this author and his work before we be called to throw aside our uncritical traditions. Surely the critics would not have us to act toward them and their discoveries as Josiah did with Hilkiah and his discovery. He was very uncritical, very credulous, in fact very stupid, if the critics be right. How did this book commend itself? What evidence was produced of its authenticity and genuineness? Where, when, by whom, was it written? How did it come into the temple? When was the truth about its authorship lost? How did it ever come to be regarded as the work of Moses? Can the critics give us no better answer than merely to tell us, It was all natural, quite natural, it requires no explantion; the author naturally presents his views in dramatic form in the mouth of Moses : all Hebrew history is anonymous, and of course a scribe would naturally leap to the conclusion that it was really the work of Moses! All that any one can reasonably be expected to do, when brought face to face with such profound methods of " explaining difficulties which the older exegesis sought only to explain away," when he meets with such a thorough exposure of the " old-fashioned plan of making arbitrary assumptions "— all that any one can reasonably be expected to do in such a case is, in all humility and with all respect, to follow the example of good old Dominie Sampson, who swung his arms like a windmill, and shouted, " Prodigious !"

VIII.—CRITICISM AND INSPIRATION.

Questions of criticism may be undecided, and opinions may vary; but the doctrine of the Inspiration of the Scriptures is held as settled, and *no critical views can be tolerated which are not consistent with it.* On this point, we should suppose, all parties are agreed; and the main question in this connection is whether Professor Smith's opinions are compatible with the Church's doctrine of Inspiration, or to use the language of the College Sub-Committee,* " the question arises whether in themselves, or in their plain tendency, they do not imperil the faith in the inspiration and trustworthiness of the Scriptures, and do not suggest views inconsistent with these attributes."

It is fair that allowance should be made, *quantum valeat*, for the element of *novelty.* Not, of course, that the views promulgated are either novel

* College Com. Report, App. I. p. 14.

or original, for they are neither ; but the combination of these views with a *bona fide* adherence to the received doctrine of Revelation and Inspiration is certainly a novelty. Meanwhile, of course, Professor Smith must receive credit for holding the doctrine of the Church on the Inspiration of the Scriptures along with the critical results which he has promulgated. But that does not affect the question as to the relative bearing of these doctrines and these results, and their consistency with each other. Doctrines may be promulgated whose logical results reach farther than their promulgators are aware of ; and such we believe to be the case here. The *teaching* is dangerous and unsettling in its tendency ; the *teacher* is apparently too short-sighted, and by some defect in his mental constitution too one-sided, to see that it is so.

1. It has struck many ordinary uncritical but fairly intelligent and sensible people, as a very remarkable thing that a professor in the Free Church should have sat down to write an article for an encyclopædia on the word "Bible," with the distinct understanding and firm resolution that he was quietly and deliberately to ignore the divine side of its authorship ; and Professor Smith in his explanation to the College Committee does nothing to remove the impression of incongruity and unseemliness. If "everything of the nature of constructive theology" had to be excluded in the sense of allowing him to say anything he chose about the Bible as a *human* book, but nothing whatever about it as a *divine* book, then the ordinary Christian conscience will have little difficulty in deciding, and that very emphatically, that loyalty to the truth demanded, that under such insulting and unchristian limitations, from whatever quarter they came, the work ought to have been declined as one which, in the very nature of the case, would give a very unfair and inadequate representation of what the Bible really is.

It is amazing that Professor Smith should regard this matter so complacently : to many minds it suggests an unfitness for dealing with the question of the Bible and all its details, which no amount of learning or critical acumen could obviate. It is a question which many find a great difficulty in answering satisfactorily how one who professes to receive the Bible as a living word from God to the race and to himself personally, could have deliberately acted on the plan which he had laid down, and how he could have so complacently carried out his own plan in the whole tone and spirit of his work. To our mind this invalidates greatly any conclusions to which Professor Smith may have come, and gives us more confidence in dealing even with his criticism itself ; for if he could bring himself *in limine* to adopt such a method, we are free to question with less restraint his whole conclusions.

2. Criticism cannot be a sure guide unless it be pervaded with a sense of the Divine authorship of the Scriptures. It is said that critics have to do only with the human aspects of the question, and inspiration must be left out of view in order that they may deal impartially with their own proper department. The very reverse is the fact. The Bible *is* the Word of God, and any criticism which ignores or sets aside that fact is incompetent ; any critic who deliberately allows it to be forgotten is adopting a method which can only vitiate his whole work.

Atheists and infidels tell us that we must argue the questions of God's being and Christ's mission impartially, by allowing ourselves to be in a state of neutrality or indifference as to which side of the argument shall carry the day. As if *that* were a proper frame of mind, a higher or more desirable attitude towards such questions! Similarly the critics, when they insist upon dealing with the books of the Bible as with *mere* human writings, manifest an attitude towards the Word of God which we can by no means regard as well fitted to secure accuracy in their results. We cannot all be critics, but we know that the Bible is the Word of God, and that all candid and competent criticism will tend to confirm this fact, and to produce greater reverence and more unreserved submission to it as such. All the more on this account will we be cautious in accepting the verdict of the critics. We will inquire well who they are, what attitude they assume, what plan they propose, what postulates they start from, and whether their purpose is to increase our knowledge of the Word and Ways of God, or merely to exercise their skill in useless speculation; we must be satisfied that those who volunteer to be our guides are really competent for the task.

Scholarship in human literature may be one important qualification; a humble childlike acceptance of the inspired Word of God as authoritative over themselves and their work, and a hearty submission to it, is certainly a no less essential requisite. Personal salvation and fellowship with God are the *highest* ends of Bible study, to which all other labour is secondary and subordinate; and when the merely intellectual and literary is elevated into the highest place, there is such a gross and glaring perversion that nothing can be secure.* And much of the more recent criticism has been of this character; the critics have been largely unspiritual men, who have confounded intellectual activity with spiritual growth, and who have stigmatised as mere uncritical tradition those views which have looked mainly to the divine authorship of Scripture, although such uncritical students have really understood the Bible better, what it is, and what it is intended for, than the most scholarly of the new school of critics. The higher criticism has not unfrequently adopted conclusions hostile to orthodox beliefs, because heterodox beliefs have misled the critics. Professor Smith has too implicitly followed this school; while he disavows all sympathy with their negative or destructive designs, he has not brought into the foreground the only efficient counteracting element, viz., the divine authorship of the Bible, which all really valuable criticism confirms. His work is, to say the least, extremely defective in holding back those aspects of the Biblical authorship which are really its distinctive feature. It has been said in his defence that that is a poor faith which needs to be for ever calling out, "I am here," as if that had any relevancy to the case. It might, with great force, be replied that that is a much poorer faith which no one can see, and that in the very circumstances in which, if ever, we would expect it to be distinctly visible.

3. Professor Smith sees and very imperfectly answers the objection, that his criticism, though assuming the reality of a divine Revelation and acknowledging the authority of the Record, "tends to bring down the notion of Revelation to a lower platform, and to make the distinction between the Word of God and the word of man less palpable." The objection is well-founded, and expresses one of the dangerous tendencies

---

* Dr S. Davidson tells us that the question of the Canon is not yet settled; what is wanted in order to settle it satisfactorily is a rational historic criticism which does not believe in the supernatural inspiration of the books, nor their direct reference to the work of salvation. (Canon, 182, 185.)

of his critical opinions. But he has a reply to it. The contrast, he says, between belief in Revelation and unbelief is absolute. " Belief says that God first finds and chooses man ; unbelief says that man first finds and chooses God ; the critic has no middle ground between these two positions." Now this may be quite true, but it is certainly quite irrelevant ; it does not give us any information about the character of the Record ; it does not, apparently, hinder the critic who believes in Revelation from adopting precisely the same views of the Record as the critic who disbelieves ; and therefore it avails nothing to tell us that there is no middle ground. There may be a great gulf between them, but if the critic on the one side can *leap* to conclusions which lie on the other, what does it matter ? You may have a clear perception of the distinction between *meum* and *tuum*, you may assure me that the distinction is absolute, and that there is no middle ground, and yet you may at the same time propound doctrines which make the distinction less palpable in regard to any particular case, " so that unbelievers [= dishonest persons] have now an easier task when they try to obliterate the distinction altogether." Your fine definitions therefore go for nothing. Surely one may well doubt (and Professor Smith ought not to be surprised at the doubt) whether such views as he has promulgated about Deuteronomy, prophecy, Canticles, and even the Gospels, tend to elevate or lower our views of the Bible as a divine book, to confirm or call in question its divine inspiration. If Deuteronomy be a mere fiction, can it also be inspired ? If Canticles be a mere sensuous love-song, can it be inspired ? And, if so, what is the great spiritual revelation of which it contains the record ? The remarkable phrase to which Dr Begg called attention at the Commission, that the deletion of this book from the Canon was "*providentially averted by the allegorical theory*," seems to imply that Professor Smith doubts its canonicity ; at least, he virtually declares that had it not been for the mistake of regarding it as an allegory, it would never have been admitted. We believe the sanctified common sense of the Church would rather agree to reject it from the canon than to receive it on Professor Smith's terms. Here, at least, there can be no middle position ; if it is inspired, it must contain some divine truth, and be worthy of its place. If you take from it every-thing which makes it really worthy of a place in the canon, and yet leave it there as an inspired work, you may say what you will about the absolute distinction between Belief in Revelation and Unbelief, but your own view of what Inspiration and Revelation are must be very low and inadequate. Probably, it was the mistake of the Hebrew Scribe in attributing Deuter-onomy to Moses that providentially averted its deletion too ! And we suspect that Ezra, Nehemiah, and their coadjutors had not heard that prophecy was a mere evolution of the spirit of the age, otherwise they too might have acted differently ! Blissful ignorance ! If these ancient worthies had known what these books really were, we would have been left without a Bible ! How thankful we ought to be that we are not critics ; we can really believe in the old-fashioned doctrine of inspiration, without troubling ourselves overmuch about the human authors ; and we do not feel in the least grateful to the critics for making a muddle of the latter in order, as it seems, that they may make a muddle of the former too.

The main difference, as it appears to us, between Professor Smith and the negative school generally is simply this. Having arrived at the same

44

conclusions, *they* say these conclusions prove that there is no special inspiration, no divine hand in these books; while *he* says, these conclusions are undoubtedly correct, yet we may conceive of God having inspired these books after this manner. Believing Theology agrees with the negative critics that either their critical conclusions or else the divine inspiration of the Scriptures must be given up. There is no middle ground for Professor Smith, and he attempts to stand with one foot on the Evangelical Theology and the other on the negative criticism. The experiment will probably not succeed, but we cannot forecast what the precise result may be.

Others also we find assuming awkward positions, which appear to us inconsistent, and which it must be impossible permanently to occupy. Professor Macgregor, *e.g.*, considers the question about the Mosaic authorship of the Pentateuch as one "not of abstruse scholarship, but of morality," * and that any one personating Moses would probably have been stoned as a profane person; he is strongly of opinion that Christ was completely committed to the Mosaic authorship, and he regards it as "inconceivable that *God* should have inspired or authorised any man to put on *the false face* of the supposed impersonation." But then again, he tells us that, if we insist upon all this, we run the risk of driving some men into infidelity! that we must not only permit but encourage the new teaching—no doubt, under the plausible guise of "scholarly inquiry"—otherwise we will do "enormous damage to the Christian cause in the rising generation"! If we ask, in alarm and amazement: How so? we are told that "the question is exercising the minds of our young people, and must exercise it more and more until the question is definitively settled in the way of real ascertainment"—all which is a mere hallucination; our young people are not greatly exercised about anything of the kind. There is much exercise of another sort among others than our young people in the Church at present.

4. We have formerly observed that the mere human authorship of a book is of little moment, provided its contents are not thereby affected. The Epistle to the Hebrews may furnish an illustration of this: the authorship is not yet determined, probably never will be, but the contents are not thereby touched. It is very different with Deuteronomy. If Professor Smith's view of the authorship be correct, then the contents of the book are in reality quite different from what they seem to be. We can easily suppose that inspired books may have been lost, having had a temporary use, which being served, their preservation was no longer necessary. Many of the words of the prophets, and of our Lord's own words, which were practically equivalent to inspired writings, were not recorded, and so were lost. We can easily suppose that inspired writers could gather their materials from other works of an uninspired character. But it is a totally different thing to hold that men may have been guided by the Divine Spirit to make use of methods which spiritual men, *i.e.*, men taught by the Spirit, consider questionable in point of honesty, and which have undoubtedly been misleading in point of fact. If inspired men were not critics, they were certainly much superior to most critics in their sense of what the truth of God required at their hands.

We repeat that no criticism is worthy of notice, because in the nature of the case it must be false or misleading, which does not tend to exalt

* "British and Foreign Evangelical Review," April 1877.

our views of the Bible as the Word of God. The human element is variable and uncertain, the divine element is fixed and unchangeable ; the former must be kept in subordination to, and in harmony with, the latter. Any views of the human authorship which are inconsistent with the most complete acceptance of the veracity, honesty, accuracy, and entire truthfulness of the contents tend to cast discredit on the divine authorship, under whatever plausible forms and phrases these views may be promulgated. It is most probable that in many cases the human authorship has been providentially kept out of our sight in order to keep before us the higher and essential fact of their divine authorship. When an author has remained unknown till now, it is about as useless to search for him as it would be to institute a search for the grave of Moses.

5. The faith of the Church in the Word of God does not stand in the literary and intellectual methods and results of criticism, but in the witness of the Holy Spirit. It is not as the words of men, but as the Word of God that we have faith in it. Professor Smith appears to us to have strangely misunderstood this basis of faith. In his statement to the Free Church College Committee he says :—" I am convinced that there is nothing in what I have written to touch a faith which moves in the lines of sound Protestant doctrine and rests on the basis indicated in the first chapter of our *Confession ;* and I cannot be answerable for the effect of my teaching on men whose belief in the Bible moves in other lines and rests on other foundations." Now it is strange that Professor Smith does not seem for a moment to have doubted or hesitated as to the correctness of his position, even when the most matured experience probably to be found in the Church plainly told him that he was moving in a dangerous direction : the members of the College Committee evidently *were* " touched " in some way by his teaching ; but he quite confidently assures them that if so, their faith must be moving in wrong lines, and not according to the basis indicated in the *Confession !* Probably the Professor did not see the manifest application of his words, and probably the Committee received them with a smile. But what can Professor Smith mean by this strange explanation. The *Confession* declares that the authority of the holy Scripture, for which it ought to be believed and obeyed, dependeth not upon the testimony of any man or church, but wholly upon God the author thereof ; and therefore it is to be received because it is the Word of God. This is the line in which faith must move, and the basis on which it must stand. But Professor Smith deals with the human authorship in such a way as to obscure the divine element, and in some cases to suggest to many minds the question whether such writings so composed can possibly have been inspired by the God of truth, to whom every shade and semblance of falsehood is an abhorrence. And yet he is convinced that if any feel aggrieved their faith must be on a wrong basis ! Why, it is just because they see far more clearly than himself that, if he be right, the true basis of faith is in danger of being shaken, that they feel aggrieved. Not that they have any real fear for their faith or its basis : they know that the Bible is the inspired Word of God, and therefore the low and dishonouring views of it which the critics advocate cannot possibly be true.

6. The inspiration of the Scriptures being established on its own proper evidence, and being an article of faith in the Churches, it must be assumed in *all* our dealings with those Scriptures. We are guilty of

irreverence and profanity if, for *any purpose whatever*, we deal with them as mere human writings. The recognition of the Divine elements in the Record is as essential to a scientific criticism as the recognition of a Divine revelation in the matter recorded. Professor Smith says truly that his criticism is not rationalistic; he admits a supernatural element in the Bible. Refuse to own a Divine revelation in the Bible, and criticism is reduced to a chaos. But while the new criticism acknowledges to a certain extent a Divine revelation, we insist upon its acknowledging also, and to the very fullest extent, the divine authorship of the record in which that revelation is contained, and we deny the competency of any criticism which does not do so. Like the Incarnate Word, the written Word is both divine and human, and there can be nothing in the humanity of it which is morally incompatible with its divinity. On one point, which is really the point round which the whole controversy turns, we cordially agree with Professor Smeaton : "An attack on the genuineness and authority of Scripture, whether dignified by the title of the higher criticism, or prompted by the lower scepticism, ought never to be permitted within the Church on the part of any office-bearer." Professor Smith, of course, does not see that his own views have any such tendency as here suggested, but the College Committee have told him that they are "dangerous and unsettling" in this very direction, and in this opinion we think all competent, candid, and impartial judges must concur.

We trust that Professor Smith himself is yet open to new light upon the subject, and that he will be led to see the dangerous nature of the path in which he has been walking. If he would consider dispassionately who they are who most clamorously applaud, and who on the other hand most seriously disapprove, he would surely, at least, begin to doubt and review his own position. Possibly he might see no cause to alter or retract anything that he has written ; and he will, no doubt, in that case manifest the courage of his convictions. For every man's guidance conscience is supreme ; but it guides rightly or wrongly, according to its light. The conscience of the Church also is supreme, and we have no doubt that the Church, when called upon in the exercise of its duty to give a deliberate judgment upon the questions involved, will give no uncertain sound, but will declare—perhaps more emphatically and with less reserve than the College Committee,—that the new teaching has given reasonable ground for anxiety and suspicion, and that in its nature and tendency it is dangerous and misleading.

DR MARCUS DODS ON INSPIRATION.*

We are at a loss to understand what can have been the author's motive either in preaching or publishing this sermon, or what good purpose he expected to serve by it. It contains some things which are undoubtedly sound and good, but it says them with no very marked insight or adaptation to present questions. The same things have often been said before : they are generally understood and accepted ; there is no special call to say them at present ; and if there was, they should have been said better than they are. The Bible, we are told, gives us the best and highest views of God to be anywhere found. " It is not pretended that there is any higher, worthier idea of God present to the mind of the most disciplined or spiritual thinker than just that idea which the Bible conveys." " Revelation is different from speculation, from a natural development of national thought, institutions, and literature. It is not man, by searching, striving to find out God ; it is God presenting himself before man." Very true, but very commonplace ; and, so far as we can see, this is about the whole truth that the sermon contains.

It contains, even in relation to this question of revelation, some things with which we can by no means agree. We are told, for example, that the Bible differs from the sacred writings of other religious systems mainly in this, that it " professes to be an account of the whole series of revelations which God has made of His nature and relation to our race ;" that in other respects there is not much difference ; these other writings contain admirable hymns and prayers, and a moral teaching " little, if at all, inferior to that contained in" the Bible.

Now, this we hold to be a gross misrepresentation of the true state of the case. The moral teaching of false systems is no more like that of the Bible than their representation of God is like the God of the Bible. There may be occasional gems of moral truth buried in the rubbish, but the mass is rubbish. An occasional detail of morality is of little value without a living root of moral principle ; and without a true conception of God this is impossible. Take, for instance, the supreme divinity of Hinduism as represented in the Vedas and the Vedanta, and you find the boasted sublimity of Hindu theism disappear before a nearer inspection. We are told by Dr Duff † that, " with one or two exceptions, all the attributes ascribed to him' might, with almost equal propriety, be predicated of infinite space or of infinite time. . . . There is not the remotest allusion to a singe *moral* attribute. . . But, if no moral attributes can be predicated of the Divine Being, how can men, constituted as they are, regard Him with moral sentiment ? " How can the morality of such a system be spoken of as little inferior to that of the Bible ? Even, if here and there a few scattered precepts may be found of a purer and higher moral parentage, yet the bloody and brutal rites of the popular idolatry, and the total extinction of all humanity which it entails, shew us the morality with which such theology is really allied.

And who knows how much of what is really good in these books may

* " Revelation and Inspiration : The Historical Books of Scripture." A Sermon. By Marcus Dods, D.D.
† " India and India Missions," pp. 57, 58.

be derived from the Bible or learned from those who were acquainted with it? Everybody knows that Mohammed was indebted for much both of his theology and morality to our Scriptures. If the Biblical representation of human nature be correct, it would be very strange if these systems were—as they admittedly are—so radically wrong in their views of God, and yet so nearly right as to the duty which God requireth of man. Dr Dods himself recognises the wide difference between the writings of David, Isaiah, and Paul, and those of the best thinkers of the heathen world ; and this distinction is as wide in reference to their respective ethics as it is in their theology.

To Dr Dods' representation of Revelation, as considered in itself, we make objection on two grounds :—

1. He makes an unwarrantable distinction between the historical books and the other writings—the Psalms, prophecies, and doctrinal treatises. In the latter, he says, the revelation is more obscure. He selects the simpler first, in order, he says, to shew how Revelation and Inspiration work conjointly ; and he intends, it would appear, subsequently to apply the same experiment to the more difficult books. We can see no ground for this distinction as regards the obscurity and simplicity of Revelation. Some revelations, it appears to us, could not possibly be given *to men as men* without being given inwardly, and Dr Dods appears to forget his own distinction between the matter of the Revelation and the record of it. He appears also to confound the intellectual apprehension of an idea with the spiritual apprehension of it. The natural man, we must bear in mind in discussing this whole question, receiveth not the things of the Spirit of God, in whatever way they may be revealed.

2. He applies an erroneous test to the accuracy of the writers. It is briefly this. A father receiving photographs of his child who is in a distant land would know them to be false representations unless they indicated an advance in age from time to time ; a boy of twelve must be misrepresented if he looks younger than when he was ten. In like manner, it is said, we can verify the representations of God given us in the Bible because they "are in a regular progression." This is a very unsafe and unsatisfactory method. For (1) it presupposes an accurate *a priori* knowledge on our part of the nature of this progression and the order of it, which we not only do not possess, but of which we are *entirely* ignorant. The father knows something about the growth of children besides his own ; but we have no progressive revelation prior to the Bible. We would thus be constituted judges in a case which is wholly beyond our competency. And (2) even with this revelation in our hands, it is impossible for us to tabulate the progressive revelations in such a manner as to show an organic development. For who can tell whether such a process ought to start with, and grow out of, a manifestation of divine power or wisdom, goodness or holiness, justice or mercy? Which is first, and why? Let any number of students attempt to draw up a systematic scheme of such progression, and, we will probably have as many schemes as there are persons who attempt it. But (3) the illustration is utterly fallacious, inasmuch as the child photographed is constantly changing, and the father knows that he must be so ; whereas in the other case it is not the photograph which must shew a progression, but the eye by which and the light in which it is examined. Perhaps the nearest approximation which we can make to the real state of the case is by considering how a modern

missionary going with the Bible and its completed revelation to a heathen land, and having the Word of Christ dwelling richly in his own soul, would unfold its truths and bring them to bear upon the natives. But could anyone forecast the process? Might it not be done in many ways? If Dr Dods' Exposition of Revelation is unsatisfactory, his treatment of Inspiration is much more so. We are indeed put upon our guard, before he deals directly with this doctrine, by the conclusion he draws from the fact that the Bible contains, and is intended to contain, simply a revelation of God's character and His relation to our race. *We must not*, he says, *expect it to teach anything else;* and this is so explained as to imply that it may contain *false and erroneous teaching on all other matters,* such as history, geography, chronology, or any of the sciences. "It has been found imperfectly informed." "Errors and imperfections have been pointed out." "Paul was occasionally wrong in a date." Now if the author meant nothing more than that Biblical writers did not always use the accurate phraseology and technical terms of modern science, that they used the modes of speech current in their own circle for the expression of ideas, as they spoke of the sun rising and setting:—If this was all that he meant, it is extremely ill advised to put it in the way he has done, which certainly suggests much more serious error as being quite compatible with his view of inspiration. And we think there can be little doubt but he does mean more. He dwells with needless emphasis on the human aspect of the authorship, the necessity of personal knowledge, the honesty and credibility of the writers as eye-witnesses of what they record. There was no special need, so far as we know, for insisting upon this at present, and Dr Dods has really nothing new or fresh to say upon the subject.

No doubt the strong prominence which he gives to the necessity of personal knowledge on the part of the Apostles, and other Scriptural writers, might be regarded with satisfaction as a set-off to Professor Smith's unfounded notion that the synoptical Gospels are non-Apostolic digests of mere Apostolical tradition, but he is careful to assure us that he has no such meaning. "We find," he tells us, "the historical writers of Scripture asserting that the prime requisite is knowledge of these facts at first hand." But these "historical writers" are not necessarily "those who brought the books into their final shape, but those, whoever they were, who first recorded the revelations made." How, then, do we know that those writers ever made any such assertion? Where are these assertions of the original writers to be found, if they are not the same as those who wrote the books as we have them? Whatever assertions we have on the subject are those of the final writers, and if Professor Smith's notion of non-Apostolic digests be correct, Dr Dods' idea of the essential importance of personal information is manifestly wrong. But it is merely playing with an important subject to tell us with so much circumstantiality and emphasis what is necessary to constitute an inspired writer, and then, in a footnote, to explain away all that is said by the intimation that it is not always applicable to those whom we regard as the writers, but to certain ideal personages nobody knows anything about. The *original* historical writers must have their knowledge at first hand, and the knowledge of Revelation at first hand is Inspiration. But, it seems, those who put the books into their *final* shape need not have such knowledge; how

D

then can we call *them* inspired? The true inspired original Scriptures would seem, on this theory, to have been lost, or greatly adulterated by the improvements of uninspired writers!

Dr Dods, moreover, contradicts himself; for while he insists upon the necessity of information at first hand as the prime requisite, he yet speaks of the writers using records in which errors existed, and documents in which facts were misstated; and of the writers of the Gospel narrative, he tells us that "they saw it and tell us of it. They were, above all else, eye-witnesses. And therefore no subsequent writers can take their place and supersede their testimony." What, then, is the use of that footnote drawing the distinction between those who first recorded the revelations and those subsequent writers who are supposed to have perfected their unfinished work? Are the Gospels the work of eye-witnesses or are they not? Are they or are they not the writings of those who received the revelations which they contained at first hand? If they are not, according to Dr Dods, they are not Scripture. But then there is Professor Smith, and the footnote!

What, then, is the bearing of all this upon Inspiration? Our author is at pains to tell us that inspiration is not mechanical, that it does not supersede the exercise of memory and the use of the eyes. "They never ask us to take their word for a thing which they had not good means of knowing in the ordinary way . . . they ask us to believe their word as honest men." All very true again, but still very commonplace, containing nothing so new, fresh, or pressing as to require the information that the author has been deeply indebted to Mr Erskine, Mr Horne, and Dr Rainy, for suggestions on the subject. These two positions (1), that the writers of Scripture were well-informed, honest, trustworthy; and (2), that inspiration did not convert them into mere writing machines, destitute of intellect, memory, and eyes—these two positions have surely been among the common-places of orthodox theology for a long time.

According to our author, inspiration apparently may be defined by three negatives and three positives. Negatively (1), it was not a process whereby men were supernaturally made acquainted with facts beyond their ordinary means of knowing (that, we believe, would be more properly called revelation); (2), it was not an influence which served them instead of eyes and memory; and (3), it furnished no means of detecting errors in the records and documents used. Positively (1), it was an influence which set them in a right attitude toward Him they were to reflect; (2), it was such an impression as moved them to preserve and perpetuate the revelation to others; and (3), it was a special influence and impression upon eye-witnesses, men who stood in a position in which no subsequent writers could stand.

After all that he says on these points, we fear Dr Dods, in attempting to explain the *modus* of inspiration, has only succeeded in shewing how incapable he, like all other men, is of doing it. We doubt if he has satisfied himself, and we should be surprised to learn that he had made the matter plain to anybody else. The nature of this influence, as we are told in Hodge's "Outlines," just as the nature of the divine operations upon the human soul in providence, in regeneration, or in sanctification, is, of course, entirely inscrutable Dr Dods appears to be somewhat conscious that he has not added materially to the elucidation of the subject, for he admits towards the close that the question, " What was that process by which Paul was enabled authoritatively to deduce a doctrinal system from the revelation made to him?" remains unanswered. He has, it seems to us, rendered this question more difficult of solution than if he had let it alone. For some of his statements on the subject are most inadequate and unsatisfactory.

1. He seems to regard the spiritual illumination of the Apostles as all the inspiration they had. They were in the right attitude toward Christ; they had His spirit; they were one with him in character and will; and thus they became the best possible channels of the Spirit; what they saw they uttered authoritatively; being merged in God, they were merely his ambassadors and spake with his authority. In support of this view our author quotes two passages from the words of Christ which have no direct reference to the question of inspiration at all, but to that spiritual illumination and fellowship which Christians as such enjoy. We are not concerned to deny that this is true of the Apostles; but it is not inspiration, otherwise every Christian may be competent to write for the Canon.* Were the Apostles perfectly enlightened and in full unbroken harmony with Christ? Surely all the Saints have the Spirit of Christ in some measure? Wherein, then, is the difference?

2. The mere impression made by the revelation received, however deep, does not constitute inspiration. Dr Dods tells us that we ourselves may have such revelations, and that we may be more deeply impressed by them than by anything we have ever read in the Bible. But, for what reason we are at a loss to understand, he does not consider this equivalent to inspiration in our case; although to *us* the impression may be such as to have all the force and freshness of a new revelation. It is quite true that our minds are already to a certain extent charged with Scripture truth, but so was Paul's before he wrote any of his Epistles; and if this were enough to close the Record, it can clearly be pleaded at any point.

3. It seems the only difference between the Apostles and us is that they stood nearest the events, and were eye-witnesses of them; but all the other influences which they had to guide them we have likewise. They were the sources, the original authorities, nothing more. Farrar's "Life of Christ" was written under the same influences as Matthew's or Mark's, except that they ["or those, whoever they were, who first recorded" the life of Christ] were nearer the events, were eye-witnesses, were more deeply impressed, and perhaps (but not certainly) had more of Christ's spirit and character.

In showing how this mode of inspiration—which is really no inspiration at all—might be applied to writings not historical, Dr Dods selects the Epistles of Paul, and, to our thinking, he is most unfortunate in his treatment both of the matter of these Epistles and the Apostle's special fitness for writing them. "In these Epistles," we are told, "he communicated to the world the knowledge that the true religion, the religion of the Spirit, had come. They teach, in a word, that Spirit supersedes law. . . . True religion is to

---

* Compare Dr S. Davidson's view of Inspiration :—"The Canon was a work of divine inspiration, because the agency of the Holy Spirit has always been with the people of God, as a principle influencing their conduct. It was not a *special* or *peculiar* act of divine inspiration." (Canon, p. 197.) The first chapter of the Confession of Faith, § VII., makes a clear distinction between the ordinary gracious illumination of the Spirit and special *inspiration.*

have one spirit with God. . . . Paul was, in point of fact, the man who saw what God meant in the revelation made in Christ." But was this a new revelation? Did God ever give a revelation in which the Spirit was not more than the letter, or the principle of obedience not more than the law? Paul saw for the first time that true religion is to have one spirit with God! This is the one grand distinctive feature of the Revelation of God in Christ! And this is the ultimate, the highest possible religious teaching! Why, the first and great commandment since the world began had been, and could never cease to be, "Thou shalt love the Lord thy God with all thy heart." That teaches what true religion is. If you call that *law*, we reply that all divine truth is law to those who hear it; and whatever you call it, it expresses the spirit of true religion. But as a representation of what Paul's Epistles teach, and what God's revelation in Christ is, it is miserably inadequate and defective.

It seems that, having discovered what Paul teaches, the question, Whether or how far he was inspired, is quite secondary. And Dr Dods proves this in a most extraordinary manner. "Put the word 'inspiration' out of Court for a while, and what remains? The fact remains that here you have the literature of the world's religious crisis . . . the ultimate and universal religion." That is to say : we would have all Paul's Epistles just as they are, whether he was inspired or not, therefore his inspiration is quite a secondary matter! We common Christians believe these Epistles to be what they are, because the writer was divinely inspired. Nothing of the sort, says Dr Dods, for *suppose* you have the Epistles without the inspiration, and the needlessness of inspiration is clearly established! Surely Dr Dods knows that evangelical theologians regard the character of the Epistles and the inspiration of the writer in the light of effect and cause. If Dr Dods had proved, what he has not attempted, that the effect had a totally different cause, then, but not till then, he might ask us to put inspiration out of court a while and examine what remains.

We might agree with Dr Dods in the declaration that "the only inspiration worth contending for is the ability to see and represent truly a revelation of God," but what *he* calls inspiration gives no such ability, otherwise every good man who writes good books is an inspired author of Canonical Scriptures. No man can be able to represent truly a revelation from God who is not supernaturally and expressly guided in the doing of it in such a way as to secure the infallible accuracy both of idea and expression, whether the matter was previously known by ordinary means or specially revealed. No amount of such spiritual illumination as is common more or less to all Christians could effect this. In the words of Dr Bannerman :* "the union of the divine and human elements, in all the integrity and perfection of each, in every portion of Scripture, guarantees the exclusion from the authorship of the sacred writings of every error and imperfection that could belong to it as man's, and the possession of all the truth and infallibility that must appertain to it as God's." The mode of inspiration it is needless for us to inquire into. It bears some such relation to the human authorship and its necessary requisites as the special work of the spirit in conversion and sanctification bears to the preaching of the gospel. The preacher uses the best method available ; he studies ; he prays ; he addresses the reason, the conscience,

* " Inspiration," p. 567.

the heart ; he uses arguments and plies motives adapted to the end in view. The result is in harmony with all this. But it is none the less a special, supernatural, divine operation which makes the Word effectual. In the conversion of a sinner you have the human and the divine co-operating in a manner analogous to the authorship of the Scriptures. All attempts to define the mode of inspiration, and bring it under the analytical power of criticism must fail, as they have always hitherto done. We can have no certain record of a divine revelation unless we have a divinely inspired record ; however good and trustworthy the writers may otherwise be, our faith can only stand in the wisdom of men.

If our faith is to be in the testimony of God, we must have not merely a divine revelation, but since that revelation comes to us in a book, it must be a divine book. As it contains a divine revelation, the Bible *contains* the Word of God ; as it is an inspired Record of that Revelation, the Bible *is* the Word of God. And all criticisms and expositions must be false and dangerous which tend to obscure its divine authorship or its divine contents. Its human authors have an exemption from error and a fulness of light which no other authors have ; in other books we *must* make allowance for ignorance and error, but in this we *dare not*. Misconception of facts and erroneous influences are quite compatible with the veracity of an historian, but not with the divine inspiration of that historian. Dr Dods says he does not care whether a man regards Paul as inspired or not, so long as he accepts his teaching. He might as well say he does not care whether a man's faith be in the testimony of God or the testimony of men, provided only he have faith !

Toward the close of his sermon, Dr Dods makes a not very intelligible attempt to distinguish faith in the Bible and faith in God. He uses several illustrations whose application is far from obvious or striking. He seems to resolve his distinction latterly into the well-known commonplace of the evangelical pulpit, the difference between historical and saving, intellectual and experimental, dead and living, faith. But this distinction is not well put when our author tells us that we must rise from "belief in Christ on the authority of Scripture to belief in Him from personal acquaintance ;" or, "the Bible has not done its work until it takes us past itself, and *makes us independent of it.*" We are not proper Christians until we are beyond and above the Bible ! If "many have so acquainted themselves with Christ that his image can never more be obliterated from their minds, nor their faith in Him destroyed by sickness, or blindness, or any disaster which might preclude them from the use of the Bible," it can only be because they have it dwelling richly in their memories and in their hearts. They may to a certain extent be independent of the printed page. But is that being independent of the Bible ? Ask these people themselves whether they have got past it, and have become independent of it. Listen to them in the Land of Beulah, on the Delectable Mountains, or in the Valley of the Shadow, and see if they have got past the Bible !

It may *sound* plausible to say that "it is not faith in itself which the Bible seeks to create as its ultimate object, but faith in God"; in reality, however, such a statement *means* just this and nothing more : I do not want you to believe *my word*, I want you to believe *myself !*

APPENDIX.

———o———

Since a greater part of the foregoing pages was in type, we have seen in the *Aberdeen Free Press* a Review of Kuenen's work on "Prophecy,"* which is understood to be from the pen of Professor Smith, and bears internal evidence of its authorship. It gives three theories of prophecy.

1. Kuenen's, which he himself calls the "modern," the "historical," the "organic" view. According to him, prophecy is merely a phenomenon in the religious development of humanity, "proceeding from God in the same sense in which everything in human life and history proceeds from him, but in no higher or more special sense." The prophets thought, or said, they were inspired, but that was a mistake or a falsehood. They had a very inadequate idea of God; in fact Kuenen has a much higher one himself, he says; and that is the reason why he does not think there is anything supernatural in their views. I, Dr A. Kuenen of Leyden, have a higher idea of God than Isaiah, Jeremiah, or Daniel; but I, Dr Kuenen, am not inspired, and have no supernatural revelations, *ergo* and *a fortiori* Isaiah, &c., had no supernatural revelations and were not inspired! Could any logic be more conclusive? Isaiah, &c., believed in a personal God, while Dr Kuenen has apparently risen to the higher sphere of pantheism, which, so far as the Bible is concerned, is equivalent to Atheism!

He of course does not believe that there is any such thing as predictive prophecy, or literal fulfilment of it. With this foregone conclusion he analyses a number of supposed predictions, and finds of course that they were not literally fulfilled, and hence concludes again that there is nothing supernatural in the prophets. Even his Reviewer, however, is obliged to admit "that he has overstrained his own case in not a few instances, and has used some violence to explain away predictions of the most striking kind." He parts from him however, "not without profitable stimulus," and with a manifest admiration of the "agreeable qualities" of his works, and specially their "unaffected candour." For our part we would consider it a sheer waste of time to inquire what such a man thought of the Word of God, however agreeable and candid his works may be. He is manifestly and ludicrously unqualified to deal with the subject. It is tolerably manifest, as his Reviewer says, that his conclusions

---

* *The Prophets and Prophecy in Israel:* An historical and critical inquiry, by Dr A. Kuenen. Translated by the Rev. A. Milroy. With an introduction by J. Muir, Esq., D.C.L. London: Longmans. 1877.

rest "on certain doctrines of religious philosophy rather than on direct historical investigations," and this religious philosophy is such as to render the philosopher wholly incompetent to speak upon the question of prophecy or any other special department of divine revelation. His treatment of the Books of Moses and Israel's history is such a caricature as might be expected from a purely deistical stand point ; and this is the man at whose feet Professor Smith delights to sit !

2. The orthodox theory, which Kuenen and his Reviewer distort and caricature in order to cast ridicule upon it. It makes " the essence of prophecy consist in the exact prediction of future events, and finds the value of prophecy for the Christian in the evidence of a supernatural revelation which the fulfilment of such prediction affords." This crass supernaturalism regards prophecy as merely "the history of future events"—" empirical events" they are called— whatever that may mean. " The measure of the supernatural is to be got by simple subtraction, by deducting everything that can be explained "—the supernatural remains. Such prophecy would not "have the slightest religious value," and is therefore " no real prophecy." And the Reviewer amuses himself with throwing stones at this *effigy* of prophecy, being apparently much more at home in casting ridicule upon it than in controverting the absurdities of Kuenen—"so acute and candid a critic "—whom he so much admires. The orthodox theory thus caricatured *is* " empirical."

3. The Reviewer's theory combines, he tells us, the supernaturalism of the orthodox school—purified, of course, from all its crassness—with the historical principles of Kuenen. By this he appears to mean that he admits the special operation of the Spirit somehow in the work of the prophets, but the result is after all very much what Kuenen says. The Reviewer gives his own opinion thus :—

" It is admitted by all competent persons, and of course by Dr Kuenen himself, that the *prophets* had quite a different conception of their work from that of the persons who define prophecy as the history of future events. According to the prophets' own account of the matter, God's word has for its function to keep Israel in sympathy—not with empirical events but—with God's transcendental plan and purpose. If the word really discharged this function, if it enabled men to walk with God in a personal fellowship of faith and love, and gave them so much insight into His purposes as was needful at each moment to cast light upon their path—if, as Isaiah puts it, the prophets and those who hearkened to their voice really heard a word behind them saying, ' This is the way, walk ye in it —then surely the prophets were justified in saying that their word was not theirs but God's."

This is regarded by the Reviewer as a higher and more worthy conception of the prophet and his work than the orthodox view—a fact which merely proves that he really does not know what that view is. It certainly involves, all that he makes prophecy to be, and a good deal more.

It may be quite true, as he says, that we *might* have " the most remarkable prediction of events verified in the most literal way by subsequent events " without any proper " revelation of the heart and purpose of God." We *might* have ! But what has such a hypothesis to do with the matter ? If predictive

prophecies do as matter of fact fill an important place in the revelations of God,
what use is there in telling us that it might be otherwise? If Dr Slade, says
the Reviewer, had foretold the price of Russian stocks, that would have been no
proof that Spiritualism is the true religion! Of course not; but is it seriously
meant that *that* illustrates accurately the common view of predictive prophecy?

The analogy of prayer is introduced, but in such a way as to confound things
that differ. "The very idea of prayer excludes such experiments" as some
men of science have proposed. But what if God himself had authorised and
ordered such experiments, as in the case of Samuel (1 Sam. xii. 16–18) and of
Elijah (1 Kings xviii. 21–39). Who ever said that predictive prophecy was a
mere human experiment? Again, the Reviewer tells us that "it is not because
we receive literal answers to individual petitions that we believe in the efficacy
of prayer. . . . The most certain answers to prayer are just those in which
God answers the spirit of our petition by denying the letter of it." Are these
two statements mutually exclusive of each other? Is either of them, taken
separately, the whole truth on the subject? Does God never grant literal
answers? Is the letter of our prayers always opposed to the spirit? Does the
habitual spirit of prayer forbid specific petitions? In all these suggested
queries we find that the illustration tells against the Reviewer. Specific predictions, we have no objection to allow, bear some such relation to the spirit of
prophecy as specific petitions bear to the spirit of prayer. But the new theory
teaches that the more we are in the spirit of prayer the less we will pray!

Any view of prophecy, to be at all adequate, must find room for many
aspects of the subject which this writer appears wholly to ignore. It must
bear in mind that the prophets and their prophecies were for *signs* to the
people as well as teachers. It must bear in mind that even to us the predictive element is no less full of present truth than the historical or didactic.
All "the powers of the world to come"—the Second Advent, the Resurrection,
the Judgment, Heaven, Hell,—belong strictly to the future. It must further
find large room for Messianic prophecies; for the preaching of Christ and Him
crucified has been the substance of all divine teaching since the world began.

We agree with the Reviewer that "we ought to remember that till we have
mastered the idea of prophecy we do not know what kind of fulfilment to
expect;" but when he tells us that "the detailed predictions are mainly
inferences drawn from higher religious convictions," we are quite sure that he
has *not* mastered the idea of prophecy.

EDINBURGH: PRINTED BY JOHN GREIG AND SON, 57 FREDERICK STREET.

SUPPLEMENTARY NOTE ON PROFESSOR SMITH'S ANSWERS.

When Professor Smith had before him the questions submitted to him by the Presbytery of Aberdeen, he had an opportunity of adopting what would have been at once a manly and a re-assuring course, viz., of expressing his deep regret and unfeigned sorrow for having been the occasion of so much disquietude to the Church, and of reconsidering, retracting, or explaining those statements and opinions which have occasioned the prevailing dissatisfaction. Had he done so to any extent, the whole matter might have been regarded very much as an ill-advised attempt on the part of Professor Smith to perform a literary task beyond his or any man's ability, in which attempt he had been misled into a number of unguarded statements expressing erroneous views, which would probably never more be heard of from the same quarter, or trouble the Church again.

The best friends of Professor Smith will most seriously lament his entire failure to take advantage of the opportunity thus presented to him, and his refusal to make any movement whatever toward allaying the reasonable and righteous dissatisfaction which prevails.

After an unreasonable complaint of being allowed so short a time to prepare his answers—although, the whole field being a subject of fresh and frequent study, days instead of weeks might have been quite sufficient—he comes forward with a series of answers which partake more of the character of haughty reproof of his questioners, and often of mere evasions of their questions, than of an earnest manly desire to be taught more perfectly and to satisfy the Church.

One series of questions he refuses altogether to answer, because, although transmitted by the Presbytery, he regards them as in various respects objectionable.

He was asked if he regarded the incidents related in the books of Jonah and Esther as authentic history. This question he declines to answer, because his reference to these books in his article "Bible" contains "no statement of personal judgment," but only reports the views of others. This we cannot but regard as an unworthy evasion, for any one reading his reference to Jonah would at once, and most naturally, conclude that he agrees with what he calls the general view, that the book of Jonah is a mere poetic fiction. He does not expressly say in the article that that is his own view, and he declines to say now whether it is or is not. Surely he would have lost nothing in the esteem of any person or party if he had been somewhat more ingenuous in the substance of his answer, and more deferential in the form he made it take. Being asked if he regards the book of Daniel as authentic history, he cannot see that the question is relevant; and so, instead of a plain candid answer, he evades it likewise. In an equally undignified manner he evades the question about the Law, by giving an irrelevant explanation about prophetic revelations and priestly ordinances, which the Presbytery did *not* want, instead of explaining the relation between the written and the oral law, which was what they *did* want. "In this question," he says, "the statement of my article seems to be incorrectly apprehended;" while he himself, either by accident or by design, clearly misapprehends the question, and succeeds under a cloud of words in saying nothing!

The only questions that Professor Smith really attempts to answer are the two regarding Deuteronomy and the Mosaic legislation. His answer to these two questions consists mainly of a restatement and expansion of his views as elsewhere expressed. His attempt to shew how these views can be harmonised with the doctrine of inspiration amounts virtually to a confession that they cannot be so harmonised. "I am entitled to believe that two truths cannot clash, even if I am not able to exhibit in a complete and conclusive manner the way in which they are to be harmonised." That is: I believe Deuteronomy is a prophetic fiction, not an historical narrative—I believe this on grounds of historical science; I believe also it is divinely inspired under the form of historical narrative, I believe this on theological grounds: therefore both articles of belief must be true! And this miserable absurdity is spoken of by Professor Smith as analogous to the relation between Divine Sovereignty and Free Will! Try it with some other books of Scripture. I believe on grounds of historical science that the Gospels are poetic fictions, and not historical narratives; I believe on theological grounds that they are divinely inspired: therefore I must be allowed to hold and to teach both! And so on through every Scripture book and Scripture character. Adam, Noah, Abram, Jacob, Moses, David, Christ, may each and all be regarded as mere poetic myths, provided only we profess that our belief rests on grounds of historical science! If this principle of antagonism between the plain meaning of inspiration and the results of criticism be once admitted, how or where can it be arrested?

Professor Smith furnishes us with several remarkable illustrations of the method in which this new principle will be applied in the Church of the future. For example, "the history of the people in the wilderness was also the statute-book of Israel, and thus there was no way of placing new laws on the statute-book except by placing them in the historical context of the old legislation." That is to say, the former laws were embodied in *true history*, and there was no way in which the Holy Ghost could reveal the new laws except by having them embodied in fiction made to look like history! "It would be very dangerous, not to say rationalistic, to reject this theory as incredible, if it can be proved historically, as critics undertake to prove, that there are post-Mosaic ordinances in the Pentateuch." It would certainly be very dangerous to reject anything which is proved to be true, but until Professor Smith adduce some better proof for his wretched imitations of Kuenen's infidel positions than he and his associates have ever yet done, he will simply make himself ridiculous by persisting in this conceited and haughty mode of speech. Surely he does not consider the whole world fools except himself—and Kuenen.

We regard these answers of Professor Smith, both in the matter and the manner of them, as fully confirming the worst impressions that had been made by the article under review. Whatever of an unsettling and dangerous tendency he has ever written he means to stand by; the discussions that have taken place have confirmed him in the confidence of his own immense superiority, and he has been raised up as a prophet to vindicate the right of all conclusions, however absurd, which profess to be based on the grounds of critical science, to the same veneration and binding power as the divine inspiration of the Word.

www.ingramcontent.com/pod-product-compliance
Lightning Source LLC
Chambersburg PA
CBHW031753090426
42739CB00008B/991